Interbank Deposits

Interbank Deposits

THE PURPOSE AND EFFECTS OF DOMESTIC BALANCES, 1934–54

Katherine Finney

1958

COLUMBIA UNIVERSITY PRESS, NEW YORK

LIBRARY OF CONGRESS CATALOG CARD NUMBER: 58-11904

PUBLISHED IN GREAT BRITAIN, CANADA, INDIA, AND PAKISTAN

BY THE OXFORD UNIVERSITY PRESS

LONDON, TORONTO, BOMBAY AND KARACHI

MANUFACTURED IN THE UNITED STATES OF AMERICA

Preface

This study was undertaken to consider the purposes which domestic interbank deposits serve, factors influencing their size and location, and the effects of bankers' balances upon monetary policy and the functioning of the commercial banking system.

Both services received by country correspondents and benefits gained by city banks have been included. For this discussion, interviews with bank officers and supervisory officials have been especially significant sources of information. Further study of the elements determining the size, location and uses of bankers' balances has been based upon statistical information. Regional differences in the significance of interbank deposits and variations among banks of different size and reserve classification have been investigated. In addition, broad movements of aggregate balances over the period from 1934 to 1954 have been analyzed in terms of such factors as gold flows and varying rates of growth among regions and classes of banks.

In examining the relation of interbank deposits to monetary policy, the effects which movements of correspondent balances have upon the distribution of reserves within the banking system have been traced. Special attention has been given to the response of bankers' balances to changes in reserve requirements. Finally, the treatment of interbank deposits in the reserve requirements of the Federal Reserve System has been considered.

The period from 1934 to 1954 is a significant one, beginning at the time of enactment of legislation (1933 and 1935) prohibiting the payment of interest on demand deposits. Such payments had previously been an important factor in correspondent banking. The study includes years of wide variation in general economic and credit conditions, ranging from depression in the 1930's to rapid expansion during the Second World War and a generally high level of activity after the war.

This study, which was undertaken during a leave of absence from Connecticut College, was greatly facilitated by a grant from the Merrill Foundation for Advancement of Financial Knowledge. I am deeply grateful to the Merrill Foundation for its financial assistance in this investigation and to the College for freeing my time.

I wish to express my appreciation of the encouragement and help of Professor B. H. Beckhart, who has been untiring in his interest and penetrating in his criticism. He has contributed much to this study; however, the views and shortcomings are my own. I am indebted to many others, too. Officers of large and small banks have been generous in answering my questions in interviews and by correspondence. Officials at the Federal Reserve Board, the Federal Deposit Insurance Corporation, the office of the Comptroller of the Currency and the New York Banking Department assisted greatly both by discussion and by providing unpublished data. Officers of Federal Reserve banks, especially the Federal Reserve Bank of New York, were helpful. I am grateful, also, for the use of the libraries at the Federal Reserve Bank of New York, Board of

Governors of the Federal Reserve System, American Bankers Association, and Chase Manhattan Bank, whose staffs were patient and persevering in locating materials for me. Finally, I want to acknowledge my indebtedness to Mrs. Elsie R. Andersen for her able secretarial and statistical assistance.

KATHERINE FINNEY

New London, Connecticut
June 1, 1958

Contents

Figures

Tables

1. Purposes and Uses of Interbank Deposits

Large interbank deposits, or bankers' balances, have been characteristic of the commercial banking system of the United States from its early years. The oldest existing interbank account is said to be that of The Bank of New York, which opened an account in a predecessor of Philadelphia's First Pennsylvania Banking and Trust Company in 1784.[1]

The intricate network of interbank deposits and of correspondent relationships reflects the historical development of banking in the United States in contrast to that in many other industrialized countries, such as the United Kingdom or France. Correspondent banking arose from two elements in the early structure of our system.[2] First, we did not establish a central bank until

---

NOTE. Foreign balances, both due to and due from foreign banks, are excluded from this study since the forces determining their behavior are quite different from those influencing domestic balances.

Time deposits are also excluded wherever possible. Demand and time deposits due to banks are usually reported separately. Published data of balances due from banks often include both time and demand accounts; however, time accounts are relatively small and their inclusion has little effect upon total balances.

1 *American Banker,* July 24, 1950. The account was still active in 1957.

2 For accounts of earlier developments see Leonard L. Watkins, *Bankers' Balances,* and Benjamin Haggott Beckhart and James G. Smith, *Sources and Movements of Funds,* Vol. II of *The New York Money Market,* ed. by B. H. Beckhart.

after 1913. Consequently, banks scattered throughout the country came to rely upon city correspondents in the financial centers for certain functions which central banks usually perform, such as the holding of reserves and the extension of credit to the commercial banks. Second, commercial banking was carried on by many independent units, rather than by nationwide branch banks or some other type of multiple office institution. With no system of branch offices through which to collect out-of-town checks or to transfer funds to and from trading centers, banks came to rely upon their correspondents for these services. Correspondents in the financial centers were the means by which investments were made, whether in the form of stock market call loans or the purchase of securities or commercial paper.

SERVICES TO THE DEPOSITING BANK

Interbank deposits, which amounted to $13.5 billion at the end of 1954, serve several purposes for the depositing banks today. Correspondent balances provide a liquid asset out of which legal reserves or vault cash may be quickly replenished. These balances are a ready source of funds to the depositing bank when the demands of its customers are heavy, and they provide an outlet for temporary surpluses. For banks which are not members of the Federal Reserve System, the city correspondent serves as a kind of central bank, regularly holding legal reserves and providing currency for the country correspondent [3] and occasionally extending credit to it. In addition, correspondent balances es-

[3] Differentiation between depositing and depositary banks is often made by designating the depositing institution as the "country" correspondent and the depositary as the "city" correspondent. These designations do not necessarily imply the Federal Reserve classification of banks for reserve requirement purposes.

tablish the relationship through which the depositing bank may obtain other services rendered by the city bank.

The collection of checks and other items is one major service frequently rendered by the city correspondent. This is especially important among the smaller commercial banks, as suggested by a sample survey conducted in 1953 among banks having assets under $7.5 million.[4] Of those replying to the questionnaire, 86 per cent reported use of their correspondents in the handling of checks and other collection items.

According to an extensive study of check collection patterns of commercial banks in 1952, about one-third of all items received for collection were sent for local clearing, about one-third were sent to Federal Reserve banks, and about one-fifth to correspondent banks.[5] However, there was wide variation in practice among banks. Smaller banks as a whole rely heavily upon their correspondents for collection of checks drawn on out-of-town banks. Country banks tend to use their correspondents more frequently than do reserve city banks in the same size group.[6]

Most banks collect checks through their correspon-

---

[4] Survey of a sample of banks made by *Banking* with the cooperation of the Country Bank Operations Commission of the American Bankers Association. Questionnaires were sent to several hundred banks. *Banking,* XLVI (October, 1953), 3, 5, 34–41.

[5] *Study of Check Collection System,* report of Joint Committee on Check Collection System to the American Bankers Association, Association of Reserve City Bankers, Conference of Presidents of the Federal Reserve Banks, June 15, 1954, p. 26. Survey information is based upon questionnaires answered by all Federal Reserve banks and branches, by most banks which had members in the Association of Reserve City Bankers, and by 598 country (member and nonmember) banks. Deposits of commercial banks responding aggregated to 52 per cent of all commercial bank deposits on June 30, 1952.

[6] *Ibid.,* pp. 36, 39.

dents. In July, 1952, checks were being sent directly to Federal Reserve banks or branches by 3,315 banks (Table 1). Since Federal Reserve and correspondent facilities are the chief alternatives for collecting out-of-town checks, we may conclude that the remaining 10,874 banks were relying upon correspondents for check collection. Furthermore, some of the banks sending to the Federal Reserve collected part of their items through correspondents.

TABLE 1. NUMBER OF BANKS SENDING CHECK COLLECTION ITEMS TO FEDERAL RESERVE BANKS AND NUMBER OF BANKS ELIGIBLE TO SEND

July, 1952

Eligibility and Sending Practice	*Number of Banks*
All commercial banks	14,189
Sending all or some items to the Federal Reserve	3,315
Not sending any items to the Federal Reserve	10,874
Not eligible to send	7,197
Eligible but not sending	3,677

Source: *Study of Check Collection System*, p. 33. Both the number eligible but not sending and the total number not sending have been computed. Nonmember clearing and member banks are eligible to send.

Smaller banks make greater use of their correspondents in check collection than do larger banks. Of the 12,000 banks with deposits of less than $7.5 million, fewer than 2,000 sent items directly to Federal Reserve banks. About 800 of the 1,800 banks with deposits of $7.5 to $25 million dollars sent items to the Federal Reserve, as did 550 of the 718 banks with deposits of over $25 million.[7] Thus five-sixths of the smaller banks relied upon their correspondents for out-of-town check collection, in contrast to about one-half and one-fourth respectively of the larger institutions.

---

[7] *Ibid.*, p. 33.

The heavy reliance of small banks upon correspondents was only partly explained by the ineligibility of the majority of them to use Federal Reserve facilities. Of the small banks that were eligible, 60 per cent actually collected through their correspondents or by other means (Table 2).

TABLE 2. NUMBER OF COMMERCIAL BANKS SENDING ITEMS TO FEDERAL RESERVE BANKS AS PER CENT OF ALL BANKS ELIGIBLE [a] BY SIZE OF BANK
July, 1952

Deposit Size Class (millions of dollars)	*Total*	*Sending* [b]	*Not Sending*
Under 7.5	100	40	60
7.5 to 24.9	100	59	41
Over 25	100	83	17
All sizes	100	48	52

Source: *Study of Check Collection System,* pp. 68 and 69. Percentages were computed.

[a] All member banks plus 253 nonmember clearing banks.

[b] Sending all types or only certain types of items and including both regular and occasional senders.

The use of correspondents was heavy as measured by the proportion of cash items as well as by the number of small banks sending. Forty-eight per cent of all items received for collection by the smaller banks were sent to correspondents (Table 3). Since 26 per cent were routed through clearing arrangements this means that about two-thirds of all out-of-town items went to the correspondent. At larger banks the proportion decreased sharply.

Many checks which are sent initially to the correspondent bank, nevertheless, eventually reach the Federal Reserve. Although smaller banks tend to send to their correspondents, the larger banks, in turn, collect through Federal Reserve banks a great part of the checks which they receive (Table 3). It is estimated, therefore, that about 75 per cent of out-of-town par items pass through Federal Reserve banks at some time in the process of collection.[8]

TABLE 3. SOURCES AND DISPOSITION OF ITEMS RECEIVED FOR COLLECTION BY COMMERCIAL BANKS ON AN AVERAGE DAY IN JULY, 1952, BY SIZE OF BANK

Percentage Distribution

	Deposit Size Class [a]					
Sources and Disposition	*Under 7.5*	*7.5 to 24.9*	*25 to 99.9*	*100 to 499.9*	*500 and over*	*Average*
Total items received	100	100	100	100	100	100
Sources						
Nonbank deposits	83	84	69	58	54	67
Deposits of banks	1	3	25	39	43	26
Cashed checks	16	12	6	4	2	7
Disposition						
Clearings [b]	26	30	34	36	40	34
Sent to drawee [c]	1	2	6	8	7	5
Sent to correspondents	48	43	22	11	5	22
Sent to Federal Reserve [d]	17	21	36	42	41	34
Miscellaneous [e]	8	3	2	3	8	5

Source: *Study of Check Collection System*, p. 27.

[a] Deposits as of June 30, 1952; size in millions of dollars.

[b] Includes local messenger presentations and some special clearing arrangements.

[c] Transit items only, including nonpar items.

[d] Includes some but not all items payable at Federal Reserve banks.

[e] County and country clearing houses, as well as various special arrangements. Includes some items payable at Federal Reserve banks.

The Federal Reserve System was established, in part, to achieve speedier and better collection of checks, and it has provided greatly improved, simplified, and quicker collection. The proportion of checks going through Federal Reserve banks has increased over the years,[9] yet many checks are still sent by banks to the city correspondent as they were in earlier days.

---

[8] *Ibid.*, p. 23.

[9] George Garvy, *The Development of Bank Debits and Clearings and Their Use in Economic Analysis* (Washington: Board of Governors of the Federal Reserve System, 1952), pp. 57–58.

The continuance of the practice of sending out-of-town checks to the correspondent is in part explained by habit,[10] in part by the greater speed and convenience of collection and by the need for other services rendered by the city bank. Greater speed may be achieved if the check being collected is drawn on the correspondent or if the city correspondent has an account with the bank upon which the check is drawn, in which case the city correspondent will then send the check directly to the paying bank. In contrast, collection through the Federal Reserve may involve sending to a second Federal Reserve bank in another district and then to the paying bank. Another element contributing to the speed of correspondent collections is the day and night transit service together with frequent dispatch or pick-up messengers to post office or airport. Many city banks send their own trucks at 15- or 30-minute intervals for prompt delivery. Air mail was adopted early by city correspondents and is extensively used today. In some cases, however, collection through the correspondent may be less speedy than through Federal Reserve banks, and the use of the correspondent may involve double handling.

Rail or other transportation connections play an important part in determining the speediest method of collecting. If a bank in central Ohio, for example, sends items to a Columbus correspondent, collection can be completed within a few hours; whereas it would take a day or more to get the items to the Federal Reserve Bank of Cleveland, after which the checks would be forwarded to the drawee banks.

10 Charles J. Bolthouse, "The Development of the System for the Clearing and Collection of Checks" (submitted in partial fulfillment of the requirements of the Graduate School of Banking of the American Institute of Banking, New Brunswick, N. J., 1939), p. 59.

Requirements concerning the sorting of checks also influence the choice of means of collection. Correspondents often require less sorting than does the Federal Reserve; [11] they sometimes require no sorting. Certain banks therefore find it convenient to send all items to their correspondents; this they can do without separating cash and noncash items or par and nonpar checks.

Quicker availability of funds may be another reason for collecting through correspondents. Federal Reserve banks defer credit for items payable outside the adjacent area, for example, the Federal Reserve Bank of New York gives credit for items payable in San Francisco two calendar days after receipt. Although city correspondents follow a variety of practice, some give immediate credit for checks received for collection. Funds are therefore more quickly available to the sending bank and, in addition, its record keeping is simplified.

In two circumstances checks cannot be collected through the Federal Reserve and are, therefore, frequently sent to a correspondent. Federal Reserve banks do not collect checks drawn on banks that are not on the Par List, nor do they collect items for nonmember nonclearing banks.

Banks not on the Par List are a small part of the banking system, and there are relatively few nonpar items. At the end of 1954, the 1,787 banks not remitting at par constituted 13 per cent of the banks upon which checks were drawn,[12] and they held only about 2 per cent of total deposits of all commercial banks.[13]

---

11 The Federal Reserve Bank of New York, for example, requires sorting by banks with a daily average of more than three hundred cash items payable outside the city or town in which the bank is located.

12 *Federal Reserve Bulletin,* February, 1955, p. 209.

13 Board of Governors of the Federal Reserve System, *Annual Report,* 1954, p. 45.

Nonpar items were less than 2 per cent of the total number of checks being handled by the banking system in 1952. About one-half of the nonpar items were collected by sending directly to the drawee banks and half were collected through correspondents.[14]

A nonmember bank may not use Federal Reserve collection facilities (unless it is a nonmember clearing bank), even though the checks it holds are drawn on members. Thus nonmember nonclearing banks, which make up half of all banks and hold less than one-seventh of total deposits, ordinarily collect out-of-town checks through their correspondents.

In addition to the collection of checks, city banks serve their correspondents by transferring funds. Customers often need funds in a specified city; for example, a buyer of feed may be requested to make payment in New York funds. He can do so by arranging with his local bank to draw on its New York correspondent or on its own account at the Federal Reserve bank. The transfer of funds can be accomplished speedily through the use of a wire service connecting several hundred banks in large cities. The bank wire not only makes possible the quick handling of transfers for a bank or its customer, but also speeds security transactions, the reporting of payment or nonpayment of notes or drafts, and other transactions and reports.

City correspondents also render important investment services to depositing banks. The city bank provides safekeeping of stock certificates and bonds for its bank customers, and it collects coupons and keeps watch over maturity and call provisions or exchange offers. In recent years, some banks have left most of their holdings of securities with their city correspondent while others

[14] *Study of Check Collection System,* p. 4.

have left Treasury obligations at a Federal Reserve bank and corporate and municipal securities at their correspondent. It is advantageous to have securities actually located in New York City or another center, since they may be sold more quickly or at a slightly better price. This is especially important in the case of Treasury bills which are turned over frequently. Furthermore, the securities can readily serve as collateral for a loan should the bank require funds from the city correspondent.

The city bank will also periodically analyze the whole investment portfolio of the depositing bank and advise concerning policies appropriate to the nature of the country bank's business. This type of service has been expanded, especially since the banking difficulties of the early 1930's.

Correspondent activities relate to loans as well as investments. City banks provide credit information and assist in the selection of commercial paper for purchase. They also help smaller banks in connection with new or unusual types of loans. They have advised concerning procedures and problems involved in establishing consumer credit departments and in making veterans', term, field warehousing, and other kinds of loans which were relatively unfamiliar to commercial bankers until recent years.

Banks sometimes seek correspondent participation in loans. A farmer in Virginia, for example, may require credit of $25,000 to buy and fatten hogs for eventual sale as Virginia hams; yet the farmer's bank may be legally limited to a loan of $15,000 to one borrower.[15]

[15] With certain specified exceptions, the legal limit on indebtedness of a single borrower to any national bank is 10 per cent of the bank's paid-in capital stock plus unimpaired surplus. Legislation applying to state banks varies and may be less restrictive.

The bank may, therefore, invite its city correspondent to participate in the loan. Likewise, participation by the city bank may be sought if seasonal increases in demand for credit within a community occur during weeks when deposits are usually low, as might be the case in agricultural regions during spring planting.[16]

Data of loan participations are not regularly available. During the first half of 1946, 112 reserve city banks participated with other banks in 1,405 loans aggregating $531 million, and their undisbursed commitments to participate in 255 loans aggregated $218 million.[17] In August, 1954, the Chase National Bank, which held a large volume of interbank deposits, reported commitments of about $110 million arranged at the request of correspondent banks for financing local enterprises.[18] Of the $5 billion in farm loans outstanding at insured commercial banks on June 30, 1956, only the relatively small amount of $80 million involved two or more banks. Although originated by about 800 banks and shared in by 400, these loans were heavily concentrated in the Kansas City district.[19]

While participations by city banks do not bulk large in the total volume of loans, they are significant in that they help banks meet the credit needs of their communities. Through its correspondent the local bank can meet peak requirements of its customers even when the demand for credit shows a highly concentrated seasonal

---

16 For a discussion of city bank participation in agricultural loans, see Edgar T. Savidge, "Interbank Relations in Financing Agriculture," *Banking*, XLVII (July, 1954), 65–68, 112.

17 W. A. McDonnell, "Correspondent Banking Plays Vital Role," *Bank News*, May 15, 1947, p. 27. Data are from a survey by the Association of Reserve City Bankers and the American Bankers Association.

18 *American Banker*, August 6, 1954.

19 *Federal Reserve Bulletin*, November, 1956, p. 1167.

pattern, and the bank can also satisfy the need of a customer who has outgrown the direct lending power of the local bank. As one bank officer put it, participation in loans by the city correspondent is "not big in dollar amount—but it is important!"

Currency shipments are another service provided by city correspondents. Other banks provide the only regular source of currency upon which nonmember banks, whether commercial or savings, can draw. Thus nonmember banks must rely upon correspondents to meet currency needs.[20]

Member banks normally obtain currency from a Federal Reserve bank or branch. This is advantageous because the Federal Reserve is the ultimate source of currency, and it is cheaper because the Federal Reserve bears the cost of shipment while the correspondent charges shipping expenses. Nevertheless, member banks sometimes do use their correspondents in order to obtain wrapped coin. The Federal Reserve wraps coin for smaller banks only, but larger banks may obtain wrapped coin from their correspondent. Occasionally a member bank may ask its correspondent to send currency rather than disturb its own reserve balance. In such a case the correspondent would likely send through the Federal Reserve.

The foreign department of the city bank also serves correspondent banks. It sells foreign exchange and keeps currently informed about exchange restrictions and import-export regulations. It will collect drafts and other items payable outside the United States and

---

20 Shipment to the nonmember bank may actually be made direct from the Federal Reserve bank of the district, but the arrangements for the shipment ordinarily must be made through a member bank.

will issue letters of credit and of introduction for use abroad. Foreign credit information is also available. Many banks require such services only occasionally rather than daily; yet these correspondent services are necessary for the occasional transaction, and they are not available through Federal Reserve banks.

With its own specialists and its experience with numerous correspondents, the city bank can give supplementary aid in dealing with a variety of operational problems. The city bank sometimes makes a general survey of procedures followed by the country correspondent. It will advise concerning machines and equipment, the physical lay-out of banking offices, or requirements for an autobank with drive-in teller service. It offers advice and information concerning taxes, auditing systems, and personnel practices. City banks are also sometimes helpful in public relations, making available the copy or art work used in their own publicity and advertising.

In addition to assistance relating to operations, city banks offer numerous miscellaneous services. Pension and group life insurance plans are set up for correspondents and information is made available concerning standard plans. In 1945 a St. Louis bank initiated a program for correspondents which were too small to be eligible for standard plans. Employees of the correspondent could be included in the group life insurance and pension plan of the St. Louis bank. This was reported as the first of its kind.[21]

City banks assist in the trust operations of their correspondents by offering general investment services and advice. A few banks have a program whereby the cor-

---

21 *Mid-Continent Banker*, November, 1945, p. 24.

respondent bank becomes a co-trustee or co-executor with the city bank.[22] This is designed to help the small bank which has trust powers but no regular trust department.

As a matter of policy or because of legal restrictions, the bank officer who requires credit himself often borrows elsewhere than at the bank of which he is an officer. He is likely to turn to the correspondent bank, where he is already known. The city bank may also render a variety of personal and miscellaneous services to officers and customers of correspondent banks. These range from the providing of world series tickets to the locating of a buyer for a herd of elephants acquired through default.

The city bank may do much to help keep officers of correspondent banks well informed. Analysis of the general economic and financial situation is made available, perhaps through monthly letters; specific information may be sent, such as regular reports of security quotations. As general informational services, numerous correspondent conferences and seminars are currently held by banks throughout the country. Attended sometimes by a small group, sometimes by more than fifteen hundred bankers, these may continue for one day or several days. Topics discussed include general ones, such as the agricultural outlook and the relation of interest rates and monetary policy, or more specialized subjects dealing with the prevention of embezzlement, loans against assigned accounts receivable, tax savings, and requirements for negotiability of instruments. In addition, such meetings, of course, acquaint the officer of the correspondent with the services of the city bank; they also widen his acquaintance with other bankers in

22 *American Banker,* March 26, 1954.

the region and so increase his access to credit information and to the experience which others have had with operating procedures.

Two further functions performed by the city correspondent should be mentioned: interbank lending and the holding of reserves of nonmember banks. Although each of these is a traditional function of a central bank, the city banks have continued to perform them in small degree for their correspondents.

Although interbank borrowing was of importance during the 1920's,[23] loans to banks greatly decreased among member banks after 1932 and continued at a low level through the war. After 1945, and especially after 1950, interbank loans rose.

The "loans to banks" of weekly reporting member banks[24] were less than $200 million on Wednesdays from 1934 through 1945, and much of the time they were well under $100 million. Their low level reflects the existence of excess reserves during most of the prewar period and the practice of adjustment of the individual bank's reserve position by the sale of Treasury obligations, whose yields were frozen during the war years. After 1946, loans to banks fluctuated widely, but at progressively higher levels; they reached $800 million in January, 1952, and $1,500 million in 1956.

Many of the loans to banks in recent years have taken place outside the correspondent relationship. Of great importance are loans consisting of the sale of Federal funds, in which one bank transfers to another a part of its reserve balance, usually for a single day. Although

---

23 See Beckhart and Smith, *Sources and Movements of Funds,* pp. 222–28 and 238–40.

24 These constitute the major part of loans to banks by all member banks.

participation of out-of-town banks has increased, purchases and sales are likely to occur between banks within New York City or within another given center. The institutions involved are ordinarily large ones.[25]

As smaller banks and those outside the financial centers have become more active in the Federal funds market, city banks have varied considerably in their policy toward Federal funds transactions with their correspondents. Some refuse to sell. Others are willing to sell even when they, in turn, must buy Federal funds for their own account. Reserves are, also, sometimes made temporarily available to correspondents through the purchase of securities with a repurchase arrangement, or through purchase for cash, which involves immediate payment instead of payment on the following day.

As another type of service, city correspondents act as depositaries of the legal reserves of commercial banks which are not members of the Federal Reserve System. State legislation requires nonmember banks to maintain reserves against their deposit liabilities,[26] but requirements vary from state to state. The general level of reserves is similar to that established for member banks; however, requirements differ greatly in reality because of the composition of reserves. Balances with depositary banks may be counted as part or, in most states, all of the required reserves. Furthermore, vault

---

[25] Hobart C. Carr, "Federal Funds," in *Money Market Essays* (New York: Federal Reserve Bank of New York, 1952), pp. 13–16.

[26] Except in Illinois, where there is no statutory reserve requirement. Congress of the United States, Joint Committee on the Economic Report, 82d Cong., 2d Sess., *Monetary Policy and the Management of the Public Dept; Replies to Questions,* Part 1 (1952), p. 468; confirmed in December, 1956.

State member banks are exempted from state regulation provided they meet federal requirements. *Ibid.,* p. 474n.

cash may be included as reserve (except in the District of Columbia), and some states permit legal reserves to be invested in securities, especially United States Treasury obligations.

Nonmember banks maintain larger interbank balances than do member banks. Relative to deposit liabilities, nonmember holdings of balances with domestic banks were consistently higher than the balances maintained by country member banks in the period from 1934 to 1954. This reflects the presence of required reserves among the balances due to nonmember banks. Higher balances are necessary also because of lack of access to Federal Reserve banks and the consequent need of nonmember banks for correspondent services such as clearing and collection and provision of currency.

In addition to the services already mentioned, banks may gain new business through their city correspondent. When a chain store opens an outlet in an unfamiliar community or a manufacturing concern establishes a plant in a new location, the city bank in which the chain store or manufacturer has an account may well be able to influence the choice of a local bank in the new territory.

ADVANTAGES TO THE DEPOSITARY BANK

While city banks render a wide variety of services to their correspondents, they in turn gain from their correspondent relationships. In fact, competition for correspondent accounts is very keen.

A major gain to the depositary bank lies in the use of the funds of the depositing bank. One large bank with sizable correspondent balances in 1953 estimated its own total cost of servicing correspondent accounts at about 0.75 per cent of average balances. It estimated that costs for a smaller bank might run to 1 per cent or slightly more. Not all the funds in correspondent accounts are investible, because part must be set aside as required reserve, part consists of uncollected funds, and part may be withdrawn quickly. The residue, however, may be invested, and its yield may bring a net gain to the city correspondent.

Banks like to grow, as do other organizations, and correspondents may contribute to their growth. Interbank deposits in themselves constitute direct expansion, and, in addition, correspondent banks are one means by which to attract new business. Just as the city bank may recommend correspondents to its customers, so the local correspondents may recommend a city bank to their loan and deposit customers.

Partially offsetting the gains through new deposits and loans is the possibility of loss of business by the city bank because of its unwillingness to compete with correspondents. Banks often refuse to compete with correspondents. However, at the expense of losing correspondent balances, some city banks apparently have not followed such a policy.

Bankers' balances bring advantages other than the use of funds and the development of new business. Income is augmented by fees in connection with the buying and selling of securities, foreign department services and other transactions undertaken for correspondents. Interbank relations also enable the city bank to render better service to its own commercial customers. The transfer of funds is facilitated. More personal attention is brought to collection items sent by the city bank. A customer, such as a construction company which is constantly shifting the scene of its operations, may wish to arrange for the local cashing of payroll checks drawn on the city bank, and this may be more easily arranged by the city bank when it has local correspondents.

SUMMARY

Correspondent services are both numerous and significant. They reflect, in part, the legal limitation of branch banking to one state or to one section of the state and the numerical predominance of unit banks within the United States as a whole. In such a banking structure the collection of out-of-town checks and other items presents greater difficulty than in a system of nationwide branch banking. The problem of transferring funds from one region to another and the need for investment services, assistance in connection with loans, the services of the foreign department, and help with operational problems are all associated with the unit banking system. Or to put it another way, if our system were one of nationwide branch banking, many services currently rendered by the correspondent would likely be performed by the head office. Here we might mention investment advice or the handling of oversize loans.

The correspondent network has provided a means of disseminating information about the general financial situation, banking techniques, and management problems. By participation in loans and by facilitating the adoption of new types of loans, including term loans and consumer credit, city correspondents have helped make it possible for the smaller unit bank to meet local credit demands. Through activities such as interbank lending, correspondent banking has contributed to the mobility of funds from one area to another.

The necessity of unit banks to rely upon correspondents for check collection and for the transfer of funds has been eliminated, however, by the establishment of the Federal Reserve System. Improvement of collection was one objective of the Federal Reserve, and better, faster check collection has resulted. Yet many member banks, especially the smaller ones, choose to rely heavily upon their correspondents for collection of out-of-town checks. Thus there is duplication of service rendered by Federal Reserve banks and by city correspondents.

Correspondent activities reflect not only the continuance of unit banking, but also the existence of commercial banks outside the Federal Reserve System. For nonmember banks, which are a small but numerous part of the commercial banking system, correspondent services of check collection, transfer of funds, provision of currency, and holding of legal reserves are essential.

2. Volume and Distribution of Interbank Deposits

VOLUME OF INTERBANK DEPOSITS

Interbank deposits (Figure 1) were large in volume from 1934 to 1954, increasing from $4,144 million on June 30, 1934, to $13,392 million on December 31, 1954. The most rapid growth occurred before the end of 1940, when they amounted to $9,677 million.

Rising throughout most of the period, interbank deposits were, however, of less importance relative to total deposits in the later years than in the 1930's and early 1940's. Balances due to banks increased from 12 per cent of total deposit liabilities in 1934 to 15 per cent in 1939 and 1940 and then declined, fluctuating around 7 or 8 per cent in the years after 1945.

While interbank accounts amounted to 7 per cent of total deposits of all insured commercial banks on June 30, 1954, they varied greatly in importance among regions and among individual institutions. Most banks received no deposits from other banks. Yet interbank deposits ranged as high as 72 per cent of total deposits, and at 63 banks they amounted to 25 per cent or more of deposits.[1]

---

1 Federal Deposit Insurance Corporation, *Annual Report,* 1954, p. 82. These data of interbank deposits at individual banks include time accounts and balances due to foreign banks.

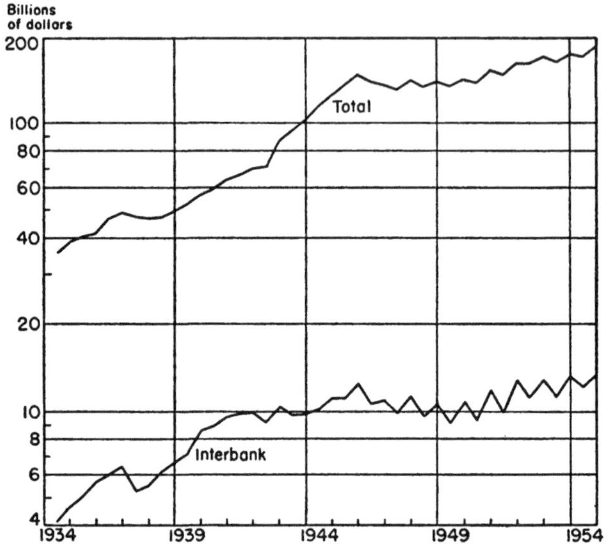

FIGURE 1. TOTAL DEPOSITS AND INTERBANK DEMAND DEPOSITS, ALL INSURED COMMERCIAL BANKS
June and December Call Dates, 1934–54

Source: Board of Governors of the Federal Reserve System, *Banking and Monetary Statistics*, and the *Federal Reserve Bulletin*. Balances due to foreign banks are excluded from interbank demand deposits. Beginning June 30, 1942, reciprocal bank balances are excluded.

DISTRIBUTION OF BALANCES BY CLASS OF BANK

Interbank balances provide a network of connections between banks. Smaller banks in the smaller centers are connected with correspondents in the nearby cities. The city correspondents in turn hold accounts among themselves and with New York and Chicago banks.

Smaller banks are likely to hold funds on deposit in one or more banks in a city nearby. For example, a bank along the coast of Maine is likely to have deposit accounts in Boston for the collection of checks, safekeeping of securities, and other services. The Maine bank may keep another account of smaller size and less activity in New York City. A bank in central Virginia may well have its chief correspondent accounts in Richmond, but it will probably carry balances in New York also and perhaps in Philadelphia or Baltimore.

Banks in larger cities, such as Boston or Richmond, in turn, maintain correspondent accounts in New York, Chicago, and other cities throughout the country, such as Atlanta, San Francisco, and St. Louis. Chicago banks place relatively small balances in other banks, but they usually carry deposits in New York City. Balances owned by New York banks are small, amounting to less than 1 per cent of total interbank deposits.

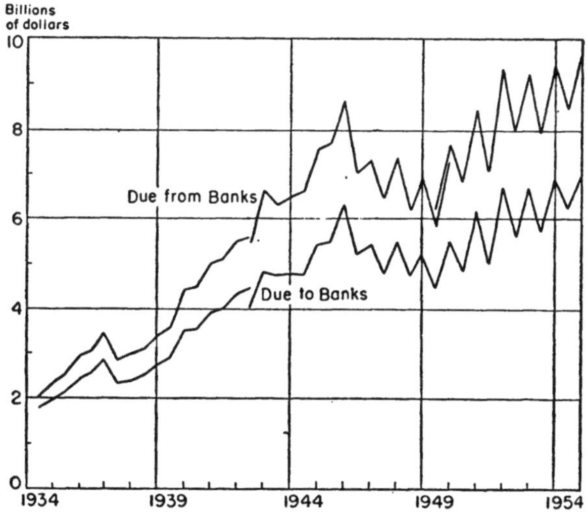

FIGURE 2. BALANCES DUE FROM BANKS OWNED BY COUNTRY MEMBER AND NONMEMBER[a] BANKS AND DEMAND DEPOSITS DUE TO BANKS AT RESERVE CITY MEMBER BANKS
June and December Call Dates, 1934–54

Source: Board of Governors of the Federal Reserve System, *Banking and Monetary Statistics,* and the *Federal Reserve Bulletin.* The sum of data for country member and nonmember banks was computed. Data refer to domestic balances only. Both demand and time accounts are included in balances due from banks. Beginning June 30, 1942, reciprocal balances are excluded.

[a] Insured nonmember commercial banks, June, 1934, to December, 1949; all nonmember commercial banks, June, 1949, to December, 1954.

That nonmember and country member banks tend to maintain their chief correspondent accounts in nearby reserve city banks is suggested by interviews and aggregate data. Officers of country banks indicated that their chief working accounts, with by far the largest dollar amounts, were carried with reserve city banks, even

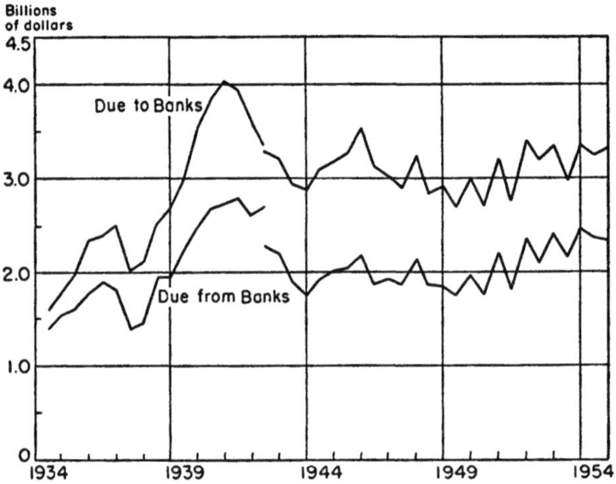

FIGURE 3. BALANCES DUE FROM BANKS OWNED BY RESERVE CITY MEMBER BANKS AND DEMAND DEPOSITS DUE TO BANKS AT NEW YORK CENTRAL RESERVE CITY MEMBER BANKS
June and December Call Dates, 1934–54

Source: Board of Governors of the Federal Reserve System, *Banking and Monetary Statistics,* and the *Federal Reserve Bulletin.* Data refer to domestic balances only. Both demand and time accounts are included in balances due from banks. Beginning June 30, 1942, reciprocal balances are excluded.

though New York or Chicago accounts were also maintained. Aggregate data suggest this relationship for the United States as a whole. Changes in balances held by nonmember and country member banks are similar to those in interbank deposit liabilities of reserve city banks (Figure 2).

In turn, reserve city banks tend to place their balances

on deposit in New York City. The similarity of movement of reserve city balances due from banks and New York City due to banks bears out this relationship (Figure 3).

At the beginning of the period, reserve city member banks were the largest holders of balances with other banks (Table 4), but during the later 1930's they were displaced by country member banks. By 1954 country banks owned 42 per cent of correspondent balances, in contrast to 22 per cent for reserve city banks. Nonmember bank balances rose greatly relative to total balances due from banks, increasing from 25 per cent in 1934 to 34 per cent in 1954.

The greater importance of country member banks as holders of balances due from banks resulted, in part,

TABLE 4. BALANCES[a] WITH DOMESTIC BANKS BY CLASS OF INSURED COMMERCIAL BANK

Five-Year Intervals at End of June, 1934 to 1954

Class of Bank	*1934*	*1939*	*1944*	*1949*	*1954*
	Amount (millions of dollars)				
Central reserve city member					
New York City	97	112	60	56	60
Chicago	162	235	179	149	154
Reserve city member	1,397	2,210	1,922	1,744	2,352
Country member	1,104	2,117	3,638	3,117	4,496
Nonmember, insured	901	1,468	2,978	2,713	3,627
Total: all insured commercial	3,661	6,142	8,776	7,777	10,688
	Percentage of Total				
Central reserve city member					
New York City	2.6	1.8	0.7	0.7	0.6
Chicago	4.4	3.8	2.0	1.9	1.4
Reserve city member	38.2	36.0	21.9	22.4	22.0
Country member	30.2	34.5	41.5	40.1	42.1
Nonmember, insured	24.6	23.9	33.9	34.9	33.9
Total: all insured commercial	100.0	100.0	100.0	100.0	100.0

Source: Board of Governors of the Federal Reserve System, *Banking and Monetary Statistics, Federal Reserve Bulletin,* and unpublished data. Percentages have been computed.

[a] Including both demand and other balances. Reciprocal balances are excluded in 1944 and thereafter.

from the more rapid growth of country banks [2] than other classes of banks during the period. This growth reflected the dispersion of economic activity from the older to the newer economic regions and from cities to suburbs.

In addition, country member banks have maintained larger balances with other banks in proportion to their own deposit liabilities than have the reserve city banks. At the beginning of the period country and reserve city banks each held balances amounting to about 30 per cent of their demand deposits adjusted, but after 1934 the ratio for country banks exceeded that for reserve city banks. The proportion dropped sharply during the war years and declined more sharply for reserve city than for country banks. In the early 1950's, balances amounted to about 7 or 8 per cent of demand deposits adjusted in reserve city banks and 13 to 15 per cent in country banks.

Balances of reserve city banks failed to keep pace with changes in balances of country member banks because of several factors. Smaller banks, traditionally, have not kept quite as fully invested as larger banks, which, with greater sums involved, can assign officers to keep hourly watch of their reserve position and others to keep in constant touch with changes in the investment market. Thus country banks have maintained larger excess reserves than banks in reserve or central reserve cities. Balances of reserve city banks turned down from June to December of 1941, a time when investments were beginning to rise sharply because of heavy wartime borrowing by the United States Treasury. Country banks

---

2 The term "country member" may be misleading to the unwary because it includes large, urban institutions as well as small, rural banks. All Federal Reserve member banks not in officially designated reserve or central reserve cities are commonly called "country" banks.

were slower in expanding their use of short-term Treasury obligations as an important secondary reserve during the period of stabilization of the government securities market.

As country member banks became increasingly important holders of interbank balances, so did commercial banks outside the Federal Reserve System. At nonmember banks, balances owned were consistently higher relative to deposit liabilities than at other classes of banks. The mid-year ratio of balances to demand deposits adjusted did fall from 46 per cent in 1934 to 26 per cent in 1954. However, this drop was not as sharp as the drop among country member or reserve city banks, and the less severe decline contributed to the increasing importance of nonmember banks as owners of bankers' balances.

Nonmember banks would be expected to carry a high level of deposits with other banks. Such balances constitute a part of the reserves required by state law and, therefore, as deposit liabilities of nonmembers expanded during the period, their required balances with other banks increased. Furthermore, as indicated earlier, nonmember banks do not ordinarily have direct access to Federal Reserve banks, and they therefore rely upon their correspondents to provide till money, to collect checks and noncash items, and to perform other services. Thus it might be expected that, as deposits expanded and as investment and loan opportunities opened up, nonmember banks would maintain balances at a higher level than other classes of banks.

The smaller size of nonmember banks is another element making for balances large relative to their deposit liabilities. More than half of the insured nonmember commercial banks have deposits of $2 million or less while only one-fifth of member banks are in this size group. Few nonmember banks are large.[3] As indicated later in this chapter, smaller banks tend to carry relatively high balances with other banks and to rely more heavily upon their correspondents for a variety of services than do larger banks. Therefore the smaller size of nonmember banks partially explains their continued heavy holding of balances throughout the period.

Thus the chief owners of interbank balances are country member and nonmember banks. Together they hold three-fourths of all balances held by commercial banks. In proportion to their own deposit liabilities, nonmember banks maintain considerably higher balances than country member banks.[4]

Mutual savings banks are another type of bank with sizable balances on deposit in commercial banks. However, their balances, which fluctuated between $650 and $850 million after 1947, appear relatively small in comparison with the $10 or $12 billion of commercial bank balances.

Turning to the distribution of amounts due to banks (demand deposits), we find that New York central reserve city banks and reserve city banks, together, held three-fourths or more of the correspondent balances throughout the period. The relative importance of the two groups changed considerably. From 1934 to 1940 interbank deposit liabilities of reserve city and New York City banks were of approximately the same dollar amount, but thereafter interbank deposits at reserve city banks moved generally upward as those in New

3 Unpublished data of the Federal Deposit Insurance Corporation relating to June 30, 1954.

4 Here interest is confined to the question of who holds balances due from domestic banks. In Chapter 4, legal reserves of member banks will be considered together with balances due from banks.

York City dropped and then leveled off (Figure 4). The differential widened. By the middle of 1954, reserve city member banks held 51 per cent of interbank deposits of all insured commercial banks, while New York banks held only 26 per cent (Table 5).

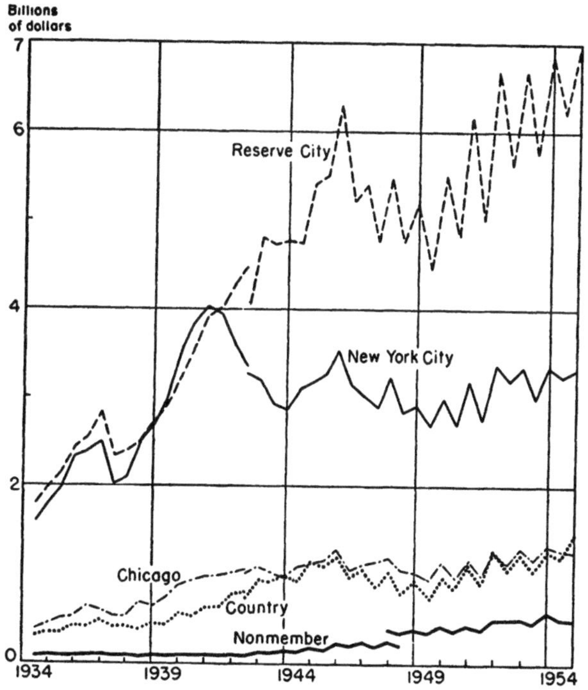

FIGURE 4. DEMAND DEPOSITS DUE TO BANKS BY CLASS OF BANK
June and December Call Dates, 1934–54

Source: Board of Governors of the Federal Reserve System, *Banking and Monetary Statistics,* and the *Federal Reserve Bulletin.* Data refer to domestic balances only. Central reserve city banks only are included in the New York City and Chicago data. From June, 1934, to June, 1948, deposits of insured nonmember commercial banks are shown; from December, 1947, to December, 1954, deposits of all nonmember commercial banks are shown. Beginning June 30, 1942, reciprocal balances are excluded.

TABLE 5. DEMAND DEPOSITS DUE TO BANKS BY CLASS OF INSURED COMMERCIAL BANK

Five-Year Intervals at End of June, 1934 to 1954

Class of Bank	*1934*	*1939*	*1944*	*1949*	*1954*
	Amount (millions of dollars)				
Central reserve city member					
New York City	1,592	2,992	3,105	2,680	3,237
Chicago	391	746	1,090	962	1,287
Reserve city member	1,785	2,920	4,757	4,460	6,220
Country member	303	439	951	762	1,211
Nonmember, insured	74	80	126	194	296
Total: all insured commercial	4,144	7,177	10,030	9,058	12,252
	Percentage of Total				
Central reserve city member					
New York City	38.4	41.7	31.0	29.6	26.4
Chicago	9.4	10.4	10.9	10.6	10.5
Reserve city member	43.1	40.7	47.4	49.2	50.8
Country member	7.3	6.1	9.5	8.4	9.9
Nonmember, insured	1.8	1.1	1.3	2.1	2.4
Total: all insured commercial	100.0	100.0	100.0	100.0	100.0

Source: Board of Governors of the Federal Reserve System, *Banking and Monetary Statistics, Federal Reserve Bulletin,* and unpublished data. Percentages were computed. Data refer to domestic balances.

Chicago central reserve city banks and country member banks have held a small proportion of total interbank deposits, each accounting for about 10 per cent in later years.

The relative decline of New York central reserve city banks as receivers of correspondent deposits reflects their general loss of position in the commercial banking field. Total deposits at New York banks, which amounted to 23 or 24 per cent of the deposits of all insured commercial banks in the early years of this study, had fallen to 15 or 16 per cent in the 1950's. This decline reflects the long-time trends of the general diffusion of industry throughout the country and the reduced importance of the nongovernmental securities markets.

The relative drop in interbank deposits at New York central reserve city banks is further explained by the reduced importance of reserve city correspondent balances. It was indicated earlier that New York City interbank deposits reflect changes in reserve city balances due from banks. Although reserve city banks, unlike the New York City banks, have grown somewhat more rapidly than commercial banks as a whole, they have sharply reduced their use of balances with other banks. Thus the relative loss of position of the New York banks in the correspondent banking field reflects both the general trend away from New York City and the failure of reserve city banks to expand their balances as their own deposit liabilities grew.

As the New York City banks have lost position as depositaries of interbank balances, reserve city banks have become more important. This reflects the growth of country member and nonmember banks, which tend to place their balances with reserve city banks. Among all commercial banks the most rapid rate of growth after 1934 occurred at country member banks, whose deposits increased from 25 per cent of total deposits of all insured commercial banks at the end of 1934 to 32 per cent in December, 1954. They make relatively heavy use of correspondent balances. Nonmember banks have just maintained their position among all insured commercial banks, but the relative size of their due from banks has not dropped as sharply as have balances owned by other banks. Thus reserve city banks have become increasingly important recipients of bankers' balances.

While a larger share of correspondent balances has gone to reserve city banks, interbank deposits as a whole have failed to expand as rapidly as other deposits. Therefore, even for reserve city banks, the due to banks has been a declining percentage of total deposit liabilities, falling from 16 per cent in 1934 to 11 per cent in June and December of 1954.

In the same way, interbank deposits at New York central reserve city banks have declined relative to total deposits. The ratio, which was 19 per cent in mid-1934, rose to more than 24 per cent in December, 1939, and declined to less than 12 per cent in 1954. The correspondent banking business in 1954 was of about the same relative importance for New York banks and for reserve city banks as a whole.

In Chicago central reserve city banks, interbank deposits have constituted a larger proportion of total deposits than in other banks. They amounted to 20 per cent at the end of June, 1934, and had dropped to 16 per cent by the end of 1954.

In summary, bankers' balances increased during the period under study but they grew less rapidly than other deposits and the rate of growth varied among different classes of banks. Amounts due from banks are now owned in large part by country members and by nonmembers, and consequently reserve city banks have become more important as recipients of bankers' balances. Due to banks has made up a decreasing part of total deposits for each of the classes of commercial banks. In addition, there have been sizable shifts in the distribution of interbank deposits from New York City to the reserve city banks throughout the country as industry and trade and finance have been diffused through the United States. Bankers' balances are much less unevenly distributed than they were in 1934.

DISTRIBUTION OF BALANCES BY SIZE OF BANK

Because of the nature of the correspondent relationship, balances tend to vary with the size of the bank. This is true whether balances are those due to or due from banks, but the patterns are inverse.

Interbank deposit liabilities are highly concentrated among the larger institutions. The 18 banks with total deposits of more than $1 billion held 36 per cent of interbank deposits on June 30, 1954 (Table 6). About 84 per cent of all interbank deposits were in the 215 banks with deposits of $100 million or more, and for these large banks interbank deposits amounted to at least 10 per cent of total deposits.

TABLE 6. DISTRIBUTION OF INTERBANK DEPOSITS BY SIZE OF INSURED COMMERCIAL [a] BANK
June 30, 1954

	Interbank Deposits [b]		*Demand Balances with Domestic Banks*	
Deposit Size Group (millions of dollars)	*As Per Cent of Aggregate Interbank Deposits*	*As Per Cent of Total Deposits*	*As Per Cent of Aggregate Balances*	*As Per Cent of Demand Deposits Adjusted*
1 or less	[c]	0.2	2.4	25.6
1 to 2	0.1	0.3	6.5	22.7
2 to 5	0.5	0.5	16.6	20.0
5 to 10	1.0	0.8	14.7	18.7
10 to 25	2.6	1.8	16.6	17.0
25 to 50	3.8	3.7	9.7	14.0
50 to 100	8.2	7.7	9.5	13.6
100 to 250	16.0	10.7	10.6	11.0
250 to 500	16.3	11.8	7.0	8.0
500 to 1,000	15.5	12.2	3.7	4.7
More than 1,000	35.9	10.0	2.7	1.3
All sizes	100.0	7.1	100.0	11.0

Source: Federal Deposit Insurance Corporation, *Annual Report,* 1954. Percentages and demand deposits adjusted were computed.

[a] All operating insured commercial banks in the United States (continental and other areas).

[b] Demand deposits due to banks in the United States.

[c] Less than .05 per cent.

The smaller banks play little part as depositaries of bankers' balances. Those with deposits of $10 million or less held only 2 per cent of all interbank deposits, although 85 per cent of insured commercial banks are in this group and their total deposit liabilities amount to 20 per cent of all deposits. For small commercial banks, other banks are not important customers.

In contrast, smaller banks, whether members of the Federal Reserve System or not, are relatively large owners of correspondent balances. Approximately 40 per cent of all bankers' balances were owned by commercial banks with deposits of $10 million or less. Among these banks, balances amounted to 19 per cent or more of demand deposits adjusted, whereas the ratio for the largest banks, with deposits of $100 million or more, ranged from 11 per cent down to about 1 per cent in banks with deposits of more than $1 billion.

In summary, interbank deposits follow a pattern of variation, increasing in importance relative to other deposits as we move from smaller to larger banks. Over 80 per cent of all interbank deposits are placed in the largest banks with total deposits of more than $100 million. Inversely, smaller banks have relatively large amounts due from banks.

DISTRIBUTION OF BALANCES BY SIZE OF CENTER

The distribution of interbank deposits and of balances due from banks by size of center in which the bank is located shows much the same pattern as does the distribution according to size of bank, since bank size tends to vary with population.[5] Interbank deposits are relatively unimportant for most banks in smaller cen-

[5] Unpublished data of the Federal Deposit Insurance Corporation relating to June 30, 1954.

ters, increasing in importance for the larger centers. On the other hand, balances due from banks are large relative to total deposits among banks in smaller centers.

Interbank deposits are of importance chiefly in institutions located in centers with population of at least 100,000, where they averaged 8 per cent or more of total deposits on June 30, 1954 (Table 7). They

TABLE 7. AMOUNTS DUE TO AND DUE FROM BANKS BY POPULATION SIZE OF CENTER

June 30, 1954

	Due to Banks [a]		Due from Banks [b]	
Size of Center (population in thousands)	*As Per Cent of Total Deposits in that Size Center*	*As Per Cent of Total Interbank Deposits*	*As Per Cent of Total Deposits in that Size Center*	*As Per Cent of Total Balances with Banks*
Under 1.0	1.5	0.7	14.9	7.4
1.0 to 2.5	0.3	0.2	13.3	9.0
2.5 to 5.0	0.6	0.3	12.3	7.7
5.0 to 10.0	1.2	0.9	10.9	9.1
10.0 to 15.0	1.0	0.4	10.9	5.2
15.0 to 25.0	2.0	1.2	9.9	6.9
25.0 to 50.0	2.2	1.8	8.6	8.3
50.0 to 100.0	4.9	4.1	8.6	8.2
100.0 to 500.0	10.4	27.7	7.3	22.3
500.0 to 2,500.0	7.8	25.6	3.1	11.7
2,500.0 or over	12.0	37.2	1.1	4.1
All sizes	7.1	100.0	6.2	100.0

Source: Computed from unpublished data supplied by the Federal Deposit Insurance Corporation and relating to all insured commercial banks.

[a] Demand deposits due to domestic banks.

[b] Demand balances due from banks in the United States.

amounted to only 1 or 2 per cent, or less, of total deposits in centers with population of less than 50,000. These averages, of course, cover wide variation between individual banks. For example, one bank [6] is located in a village with population of only 200, yet some 75

[6] National Stock Yards National Bank near St. Louis. See *Business Week,* April 21, 1956, pp. 125–26.

per cent of its $100 million of deposits come from bank correspondents.

High interbank deposits are to be expected in the larger centers since regional trading, industrial and financial activities are concentrated there. These are market places where funds are received and where funds are needed to make payment. Transportation and communication facilities required for handling correspondent business are likely to be available. Furthermore, banks of large enough size to provide correspondent services most effectively are usually located in the larger centers.

When related to total deposits, balances due from banks show an inverse distribution. As a percentage of total deposits, balances decline with increasing size of center, ranging from 15 per cent in the smallest to 1 per cent in the largest population centers.

In dollar amount, however, holdings of balances due from banks are not concentrated in the smaller centers. Only 16 per cent of all balances are owned by banks in centers with population of less than 2,500 although these banks make up more than half of all banks and in spite of their maintaining balances high in relation to their own deposit liabilities. Almost 40 per cent of balances belonged to banks in centers whose population exceeded 100,000.

CONCENTRATION OF INTERBANK DEPOSITS AMONG BANKS

The nature of correspondent banking leads to a high degree of concentration of interbank deposits within relatively few banks, and concentration is higher than in total deposits. On June 30, 1954, the largest 18 banks held 36 per cent of all demand deposits due to domestic banks as compared with 25 per cent of the total deposits of all insured commercial banks.[7] The 215 banks with deposits of over $100 million held 84 per cent of all interbank deposits in contrast to 55 per cent of total deposits.

A survey of correspondent balances by the *American Banker* in 1954 shows even greater concentration. The 10 banks with largest correspondent balances held 37 per cent of interbank deposits of all member banks, the top 20 held 50 per cent, and the top 30 held 57 per cent.[8] The degree of concentration here is higher than that indicated in the preceding paragraph because these banks were selected upon the basis of their holdings of interbank deposits and because of the inclusion of balances due to foreign banks, which are highly concentrated.

In each Federal Reserve district interbank deposits are more highly concentrated within a few banks than are total deposits. In most districts more than half of the correspondent balances were on deposit in 4 or fewer banks (Table 8),[9] while only in the San Francisco district are total deposits so highly concentrated. The degree of concentration is increased in some districts in consequence of the inclusion of time deposits and amounts due to foreign banks. The effect of this inclusion is especially great in the New York district, where foreign deposits, many of them time accounts, are largely concentrated within a few large New York City banks. In the Boston and San Francisco districts, foreign ac-

---

7 Unpublished data of the Federal Deposit Insurance Corporation.

8 Computed from *American Banker,* December 16, 1954, and *Member Bank Call Report.* Data refer to October 7, 1954.

9 Balances in leading correspondent banks are compared with interbank deposits of member banks only, because data for all commercial banks are not available by Federal Reserve district. At the end of 1954 interbank deposits (foreign and domestic) of all commercial banks exceeded those of all member banks by $825 million, or 5 per cent.

counts are likewise a significant proportion of total interbank balances.

TABLE 8. INTERBANK DEPOSITS[a] AT FOUR LEADING CORRESPONDENTS IN EACH FEDERAL RESERVE DISTRICT
October 7, 1954

District	*Amount (millions of dollars)*	*As Per Cent of Interbank Deposits of Member Banks of District*
1. Boston	346	71
2. New York	3,034	54
3. Philadelphia	414 [b]	88 [b]
4. Cleveland	335	57
5. Richmond	241	40
6. Atlanta	244	28
7. Chicago	1,251	61
8. St. Louis	456	53
9. Minneapolis	308	69
10. Kansas City	410	38
11. Dallas	543	45
12. San Francisco	521	56

Source: Compiled from *American Banker*, December 16, 1954, which obtained data by a questionnaire sent to the 400 largest commercial banks. Replies were published for 331 banks.

[a] Due to both foreign and domestic banks and including time deposits.

[b] One bank reported only domestic balances but any foreign balances thereby excluded could have little effect upon the data shown here.

In most districts more than 75 per cent of interbank deposits are placed within 11 banks or fewer. However, in the Atlanta,[10] Kansas City, and Dallas districts the percentages are lower, with 11 banks holding 63, 66, and 71 per cent, respectively, of the interbank deposits of the district. These lower percentages may reflect the incompleteness of the sample reported. However, they suggest greater dispersion of interbank deposits among smaller banks there, since the degree of concentration

[10] For the Atlanta district December 31 data were included from *Finance* (February 15, 1955) for two banks not reported in the October 7 data of *American Banker*. This probably slightly overstates the degree of concentration.

of total deposits within a few large banks is low in these districts.

The concentration of balances due to both foreign and domestic banks in 1954 did not differ significantly from that in 1944. According to *Finance* surveys, the 19 banks with the largest correspondent balances in 1954 held $7.8 billion of interbank deposits, or 47 per cent of the total for all commercial banks, as compared with $5.6 billion, or 45 per cent, for the leading 19 in 1944.[11]

In contrast to total correspondent deposits, domestic balances became somewhat more widely distributed. If foreign deposits, included in the *Finance* surveys, could be eliminated, the degree of concentration would be reduced in each year, but especially in 1954. Thus, although the degree of concentration of all correspondent balances showed little change, domestic balances were less highly concentrated in 1954 than in 1944.

In summary, for the country as a whole and for each Federal Reserve district, correspondent banking is more highly concentrated within a few banks than is banking in general. The concentration of balances due to both foreign and domestic banks remained the same in 1954 as in 1944 but fell for domestic balances.

DISTRIBUTION OF BALANCES BY FEDERAL RESERVE DISTRICT

Bankers' balances have been very unevenly distributed geographically, and striking shifts in their distribution have taken place since 1934. Interbank deposits have generally shifted away from New York City and the New England and Middle Atlantic regions toward the South, Southwest, and Middle West, and consequently they are now less unevenly spread through-

[11] Computed from *Finance,* January 25, 1945, and February 15, 1955. Data refer to the end of the year.

out the districts than they were in 1934. Balances due from banks, which have been more widely scattered than have deposits due to banks, are more unevenly distributed than formerly.

The banks of the New York Federal Reserve district have continued to receive a large part of domestic balances, with the Chicago district second in amount (Table 9). However, the position of the New York

TABLE 9. INTERBANK DEPOSITS[a] AND TOTAL DEPOSITS OF MEMBER BANKS BY FEDERAL RESERVE DISTRICT AS PER CENT OF TOTAL FOR ALL MEMBER BANKS
End of December, 1934 and 1954

	Interbank Deposits		*Total Deposits*	
District	*1934*	*1954*	*1934*	*1954*
1. Boston	4.7	3.3	6.5	4.5
2. New York	41.1	26.8	35.8	25.4
3. Philadelphia	5.7	3.8	7.0	5.1
4. Cleveland	5.1	4.5	7.8	8.0
5. Richmond	3.7	4.6	3.8	4.6
6. Atlanta	3.4	7.8	3.2	5.1
7. Chicago	13.6	14.9	12.3	16.0
8. St. Louis	4.4	7.0	3.4	3.9
9. Minneapolis	2.9	3.3	2.7	2.7
10. Kansas City	6.8	8.3	4.1	4.8
11. Dallas	3.5	11.1	3.0	5.8
12. San Francisco	5.2	4.5	10.4	14.1
All member banks	100.0	100.0	100.0	100.0

Source: Board of Governors of the Federal Reserve System, *Banking and Monetary Statistics* for 1934 and *Member Bank Call Report* for 1954. Percentages were computed.

[a] Demand deposits due to banks in the United States.

banks has declined as their holdings of interbank deposits dropped from 41 to 27 per cent of the total, while banks of the Chicago district held approximately the same proportion of interbank deposits in 1954 as in 1934. The more widespread distribution of interbank deposits has therefore reflected in considerable part the lessening of the predominance of the New York City banks and, also, the diminished importance of banks located in the Boston, Philadelphia, Cleveland, and San Francisco districts.

The shift in location of bankers' balances reflects the changing distribution of total deposits and economic activity between Federal Reserve districts. Deposits in the New York district dropped from 36 per cent of total member bank deposits in 1934 to 25 per cent in

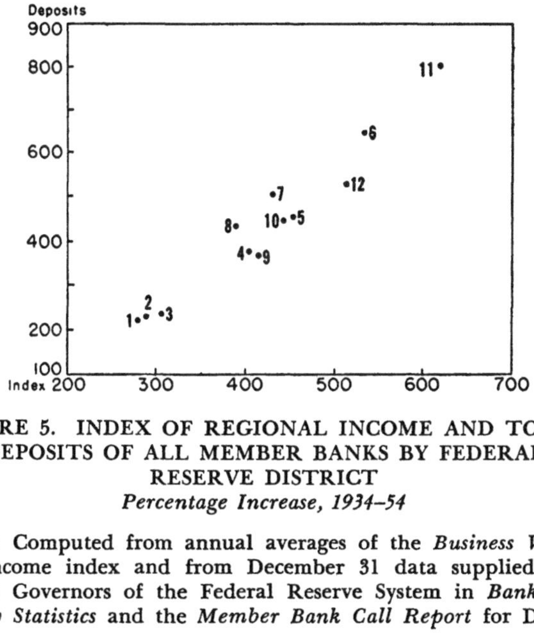

FIGURE 5. INDEX OF REGIONAL INCOME AND TOTAL DEPOSITS OF ALL MEMBER BANKS BY FEDERAL RESERVE DISTRICT

Percentage Increase, 1934–54

Source: Computed from annual averages of the *Business Week* regional income index and from December 31 data supplied by the Board of Governors of the Federal Reserve System in *Banking and Monetary Statistics* and the *Member Bank Call Report* for December 31, 1954.

1954 (Table 9). Total deposits of the Boston and Philadelphia districts also declined in relation to the country as a whole, and the Cleveland district showed only a slight increase. All other districts (except Minneapolis) gained in relative position.

Banking developments have accompanied the industrial expansion of the newer regions of the country and improvement of the agricultural situation in the past twenty years. Total deposits within districts have tended to vary with income (Figure 5). The Boston, New York and Philadelphia districts with their lower percentage increases in income show the slowest growth of total deposits. The more rapid growth of income in the

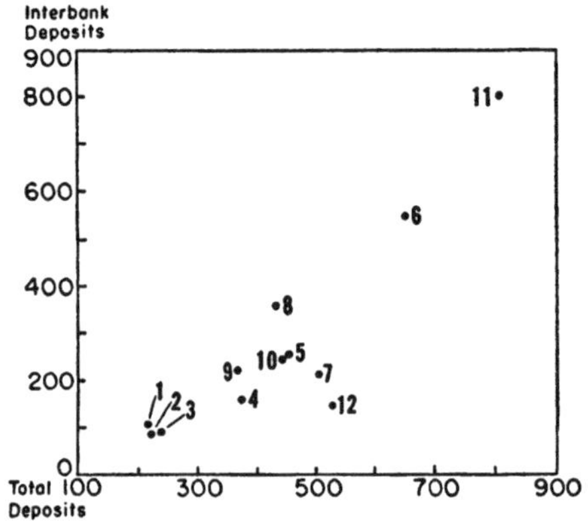

FIGURE 6. TOTAL DEPOSITS AND INTERBANK DEPOSITS[a] OF ALL MEMBER BANKS BY FEDERAL RESERVE DISTRICT
Percentage Increase, 1934–54

Source: Computed from December 31 data supplied by the Board of Governors of the Federal Reserve System in *Banking and Monetary Statistics* and the *Member Bank Call Report* for December 31, 1954.
[a] Demand deposits due to banks in the United States.

Dallas, Atlanta, and San Francisco districts brought large increases in deposits.

From the end of 1934 to the end of 1954, interbank balances and total deposits generally moved together (Figure 6). Reflecting its highly developed system of branch banking, the Twelfth (San Francisco) District was exceptional in that its interbank deposits showed less growth than the increase in its total deposits would suggest.

The decline of the older centers of correspondent

banking reflects not only the relative loss of total deposits there but also changes in the ownership of balances due from banks. Formerly large banks were the chief holders, but interbank balances are now more nearly dominated by country member and nonmember banks which tend to hold their correspondent accounts

TABLE 10. MEMBER BANK BALANCES WITH DOMESTIC BANKS BY FEDERAL RESERVE DISTRICT AS PER CENT OF TOTAL FOR ALL MEMBER BANKS

End of December, 1934 and 1954

District	*1934*	*1954*
1. Boston	5.7	3.5
2. New York	8.9	6.6
3. Philadelphia	8.0	5.2
4. Cleveland	8.6	7.0
5. Richmond	5.5	6.5
6. Atlanta	6.2	9.9
7. Chicago	16.4	15.4
8. St. Louis	5.0	6.2
9. Minneapolis	5.6	3.8
10. Kansas City	11.2	11.1
11. Dallas	7.9	17.6
12. San Francisco	11.0	7.3
All member banks	100.0	100.0

Source: Board of Governors of the Federal Reserve System, *Banking and Monetary Statistics* for 1934. Computed from *Member Bank Call Report* for 1954. All percentages were computed.

in nearby cities rather than in the more distant financial centers. Therefore a dispersion of interbank deposits has taken place.

The geographical distribution of member bank balances due from banks changed greatly during the twenty years, and these shifts, like those of interbank deposits, reflected general banking developments. Banks in the South and Southwest held increasing proportions of balances, rising from 8 to 18 per cent in the Dallas district and from 6 to 10 per cent in the Atlanta district (Table 10). Correspondingly, balances owned by banks in New England and the Middle Atlantic states and the Middle West declined in relative importance.

District increases in balances due from banks were generally associated with increases in total deposits (Figure 7). In the Dallas and Atlanta districts, where general economic expansion was unusually rapid, both total deposits and amounts due from banks grew most rapidly. As with deposits due to banks, the growth of

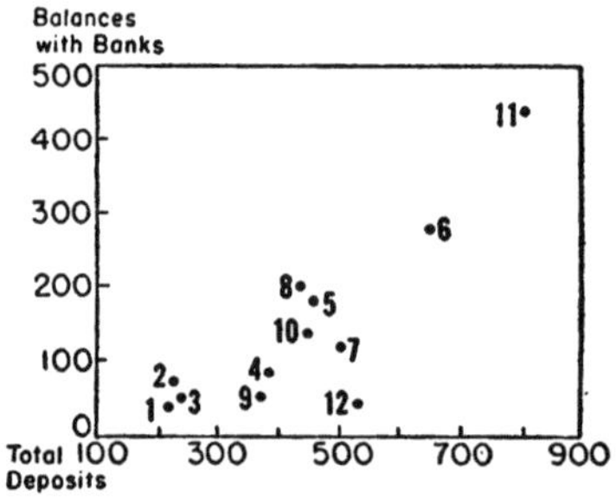

FIGURE 7. TOTAL DEPOSITS AND INTERBANK BALANCES[a] OF ALL MEMBER BANKS BY FEDERAL RESERVE DISTRICT
Percentage Increase, 1934–54

Source: Computed from December 31 data supplied by the Board of Governors of the Federal Reserve System in *Banking and Monetary Statistics* and the *Member Bank Call Report* for December 31, 1954.
[a] Demand and other balances with banks in the United States.

balances was disproportionately small in the San Francisco district.

The geographical distribution of bankers' balances is also affected by their size relative to total deposits. The ratio of interbank deposits and of balances due from banks to total deposit liabilities within the district indicates the amount of emphasis placed upon correspondent banking and measures the importance of bankers' balances in the region.

The ratio of interbank balances to total deposits

varies widely from one Federal Reserve district to another, ranging from 2 to 16 per cent (Table 11). Both due to and due from banks are high in the Dallas, St. Louis, Kansas City, Atlanta, and Minneapolis districts and low in the San Francisco, Cleveland, Boston, and Philadelphia districts.[12] In the New York district, inter-

TABLE 11. FEDERAL RESERVE DISTRICTS RANKED ACCORDING TO RATIO OF INTERBANK TO TOTAL DEPOSITS AND DEMAND BALANCES TO TOTAL DEPOSITS
December 31, 1954

District	*Interbank Deposits as Per Cent of Total Deposits* [a]	*District*	*Demand Balances with Banks in U.S. as Per Cent of Total Deposits* [b]
11. Dallas	15.8	11. Dallas	16
8. St. Louis	15.0	10. Kansas City	14
10. Kansas City	14.2	6. Atlanta	13
6. Atlanta	12.5	8. St. Louis	12
9. Minneapolis	10.2	5. Richmond	10
2. New York	8.8	9. Minneapolis	9
5. Richmond	8.4	7 Chicago	7
7. Chicago	7.7	4. Cleveland	5
3. Philadelphia	6.1	3. Philadelphia	5
1. Boston	6.1	1. Boston	5
4. Cleveland	4.7	12. San Francisco	3
12. San Francisco	2.6	2. New York	2
All districts	8.3	All districts	6

Source: Computed from *Member Bank Call Report* for December 31, 1954, and Federal Deposit Insurance Corporation Report Number 42.

[a] Member banks only. Interbank deposits do not include time and foreign deposits. Percentages are based on actual district data.

[b] All insured commercial banks. Federal Reserve districts are approximate, with no splitting of state data. Percentages are therefore approximate.

---

12 Percentages relating to deposits due to banks include member bank data only since nonmember bank data are not available by district and since the interbank deposits of nonmember banks are small ($496 million in comparison with $13,015 million for all member banks on December 31, 1954).

Ratios of balances with banks include all insured commercial banks, but district data are approximate because no attempt was made to split state data where Reserve districts cut across states. Each state is included in the district in which the major part of its deposits falls.

bank deposits are slightly above the average for all member banks and balances due from banks are low relative to total deposits.

Differences in the relation of interbank to total deposits reflect diversity in both the structure of commercial banking and the nature of economic and banking activity. In the New York district, the position of New York City as a center of domestic and international finance and of industrial and distributive activities leads to interbank deposits larger than average and also leads to low need for balances due from banks.

Districts outside New York vary widely in their structures, as evidenced by the number and size of commercial banks, by the degree of branch banking, and by membership or nonmembership in the Federal Reserve System. In districts where there are many banks, balances due from banks are high relative to total deposits (Table 12). The larger number of banks ordinarily means that many are small, and the smaller banks are the heavier owners of balances.

The number of banks also reflects the degree of development of branch banking, which varies widely throughout the United States since the establishment of branches is determined chiefly by state legislation. Extensive branch banking may wipe out correspondent accounts in large part or convert them into interoffice accounts. Thus, in the San Francisco district, where branch banking has been widely adopted, bankers' balances are relatively small. In the Dallas, Kansas City, Atlanta, St. Louis, and Minneapolis districts the number of branches outside the head office city is less than 10 per cent of the total number of banks of the district (Table 12). In each of these districts, interbank balances are relatively large. However, lack of branch banking does not explain the high balances in the Richmond district, where more than four hundred branches operate outside their head office city.

TABLE 12. NUMBER OF COMMERCIAL BANKS, NUMBER OF SMALL BANKS, AND NUMBER OF BRANCHES OUTSIDE HEAD OFFICE CITY BY FEDERAL RESERVE DISTRICT

District (in order of ratio of demand balances with banks in U.S. to total deposits)	*Number of Commercial Banks in District as Per Cent of All Districts*	*Number of Smaller Banks*[a] *Banks with Deposits of $2 Million or Less as Per Cent of District*	*Number of Smaller Banks*[a] *Banks with Deposits of $25 Million or Less as Per Cent of District*	*Number of Branches Outside Head Office City as Per Cent of Banks of District*
11. Dallas	7.6	39	94	4.3
10. Kansas City	12.8	54	98	0.2
6. Atlanta	9.0	45	95	9.8
8. St. Louis	10.6	53	97	8.0
5. Richmond	7.3	36	95	40.2
9. Minneapolis	9.3	57	98	8.4
7. Chicago	18.1	39	95	17.5
4. Cleveland	7.5	32	94	23.4
3. Philadelphia	5.7	23	94	18.7
1. Boston	3.3	17	90	59.0
12. San Francisco	3.1	24	88	287.3
2. New York	5.7	16	87	47.8
All districts	100.0	39	94	25.4

Sources: Board of Governors of the Federal Reserve System, *Annual Report,* 1954, and unpublished data of the Board of Governors and of the Federal Deposit Insurance Corporation. The number of commercial banks and branches relates to December 31, 1954, number of smaller banks to June 30, 1953.

[a] Approximate Federal Reserve districts.

The importance of interbank balances tends to vary with the proportion of banks that are outside the Federal Reserve System, and this proportion varies widely from one region to another. In the Kansas City, Atlanta, St. Louis, Richmond, and Minneapolis districts, where balances are high, nonmember banks constitute more than half the total number of commercial banks and account for more than 21 per cent of total deposits (Table 13). There are also many nonmembers in the Chicago district, where balances are higher than average.

TABLE 13. NONMEMBER COMMERCIAL BANKS AND BANKS NOT ON PAR LIST BY FEDERAL RESERVE DISTRICT
December 31, 1954

	Nonmember Banks		
District (in order of ratio of demand balances with banks in U.S. to total deposits)	*Number as Per Cent of Commercial Banks of District* [a]	*Total Deposits as Per Cent of Total Deposits of District*	*Nonpar Banks as Per Cent of Commercial Banks of District* [a]
11. Dallas	39.8	12.9	8.8
10. Kansas City	57.3	21.4	0.4
6. Atlanta	70.0	25.3	47.0
8. St. Louis	66.4	31.0	21.6
5. Richmond	52.6	27.7	18.6
9. Minneapolis	63.0	29.7	47.0
7. Chicago	59.1	17.6	...
4. Cleveland	38.6	12.2	...
3. Philadelphia	24.5	16.2	...
1. Boston	31.5	13.3	...
12. San Francisco	45.2	8.5	...
2. New York	13.6	5.4	...
All districts	51.6	14.9	13.0

Sources: Board of Governors of the Federal Reserve System, *Annual Report*, 1954, *Member Bank Call Report* for December 31, 1954, and Release E.4. Nonmember deposits were derived and all percentages computed.

[a] Included are commercial banks on which checks are drawn.

The Dallas district, with high interbank balances, is an exception since nonmember banks are of much less importance there.

Another and related factor is the proportion of banks that do not remit at par. All member banks are required to remit at par when checks drawn upon them are presented for payment, and most nonmember banks actually do remit at par. However, about eighteen hundred nonmember banks were not on the par list at the end of 1954. Checks drawn upon these banks cannot be presented through Federal Reserve banks and are often sent to a city correspondent for collection. The correspondent in turn sends directly to the nonpar bank or collects through a bank in the local area. Thus the collection of nonpar items necessitates the use of correspondent banks to a degree not true of par items.

The concentration of nonpar banks within a few districts partially explains the relative importance of bankers' balances there. High interbank deposits in the Atlanta, Minneapolis, St. Louis, and Richmond areas reflect the large number of banks in those districts which do not remit at par, and the presence of nonpar banks contributes to the high level of balances in the Dallas district (Table 13).

Thus the distribution of bankers' balances by Federal Reserve districts reflects various aspects of the banking structure. In those districts in which there is a large number of small unit banks, especially nonmember banks, or where there are large numbers of nonpar banks, the proportionate holdings of bankers' balances appear high in relation to total deposits of the district.

The type of banking business carried on within the district and the nature of economic activity within the area also affect the geographical distribution of bankers' balances. Regional differences in the relative importance of demand and time deposits are sometimes offered as an explanation of geographical variation in the relative importance of interbank deposits. Since demand deposits ordinarily show greater activity than do time deposits, banks with a smaller proportion of time deposits might be expected to hold larger balances than other banks. Member bank data for 1954 show that the ratio of time to total deposits actually is low in several districts in which balances are relatively high. The averages for individual member banks in the Dallas and Kansas City districts were 8.2 and 14.5 per cent respectively, as compared with 31.5 per cent for all member banks; the ratios in the St. Louis and Atlanta districts were also low.[13] All these are districts of high interbank balances. The Boston district is an exception, however, since time deposits there are less important than in other districts; yet, its balances due from banks are low.

The relative importance of time deposits is only one factor among many, however, in explaining the variations between districts. When interbank balances are compared with demand deposits adjusted, rather than total deposits, the same districts show higher than average balances. The Dallas, Kansas City, Atlanta, St. Louis, Minneapolis, and Richmond districts are still high. Likewise, amounts due to banks are high relative to demand deposits adjusted in the St. Louis, Dallas, Kansas City, Atlanta, Minneapolis, and New York districts. Thus the major explanation of the distribution of bankers' balances lies elsewhere than in the widely differing ratios of demand and time deposits in the various districts.

Sharpness of seasonal fluctuations of deposits is another element making for a high level of interbank deposits. This is especially significant in agricultural

[13] *Federal Reserve Bulletin*, June, 1955, p. 712.

regions where the moving of crops to market leads to an increase in total deposits and brings either an inflow of funds into the district or an increase in loans for the carrying of crops.

With the sale of agricultural products outside the farmer's comunity, the local bank receives either additional reserves at the Federal Reserve bank or balances with its correspondent. Since there is no need for building excess reserves, the local bank may well allow its correspondent balances to swell in order to compensate the city bank for services rendered throughout the year. Thus the ratio of balances on deposit at correspondent banks to total deposit liabilities rises. Such movement of balances was observed in a study of country member banks of the Kansas City district.[14]

The seasonal upswing in interbank balances resulting from agricultural marketings may be lessened, however, by an increase in loans guaranteed by the Commodity Credit Corporation, as indicated in the study of banks in the Kansas City district. If the market price is below the support level, guaranteed loans may take the place of the marketing of farm crops. Thus the country bank does not receive payment from outside the community and its due from banks does not swell.

The influence which the seasonal pattern of the marketing of farm products has upon interbank balances is heightened by the fact that banks serving agricultural communities are likely to be small. These smaller institutions make heavy use of their correspondents and adjust their reserve position through changes in balances due from banks.

---

14 "Variations in Interbank Balances," *Monthly Review* (Federal Reserve Bank of Kansas City), June, 1955, pp. 10–12.

Finance of cattle raising and procedures used in making settlement for stockyards sales have affected the relative importance of bankers' balances in the St. Louis and Kansas City districts and elsewhere. Deposits at "stockyards" banks have come in large part from bank correspondents; interbank accounts amount to 70 per cent or more of total deposits in some institutions. Services rendered by stockyards banks have been similar to those usually rendered by city correspondents, but especially important have been livestock loans too large for the smaller country banks to handle. In addition, the proceeds of livestock shipments may be credited to the correspondent account of the shipper's bank.[15] However, if stockyards banks are excluded, the Kansas City, St. Louis, and Chicago districts still rank high in holdings of bankers' balances.

Regional industrial characteristics also affect the distribution of interbank deposits. A study of the economic resources of the South[16] found a surprisingly small ownership of demand deposits by manufacturing and mining companies in the Richmond, Atlanta, and Dallas Federal Reserve districts. Although manufacturing and mining companies carried on 13 to 17 per cent of their activities in these districts, they held only 7 to 9 per cent of their deposits in banks located there. The relatively low volume of these deposits is explained chiefly by the fact that much of Southern manufacturing and mining is carried on by branches of large companies which maintain their principal deposit accounts elsewhere. In order to better serve their own "national

---

[15] Garvy, *Development of Bank Debits and Clearings,* pp. 163–64.

[16] Calvin B. Hoover and B. U. Ratchford, *Economic Resources and Policies of the South* (New York: Macmillan Co., 1951), pp. 177–78.

accounts," the banks near the corporate head offices need to maintain interbank deposits in the areas of actual operations. The textile, cotton, oil, and other industries with heavy financing requirements and interregional connections explain much of the importance of interbank balances in the South.

Another element contributing to regional differences in the development of correspondent banking is the aggressiveness with which banks have pursued interbank accounts. The vigor with which the banks of the Dallas district, for example, have sought correspondent relationships has been one element in explaining the high level of bankers' balances there.

SUMMARY

During the period from 1934 to 1954, bankers' balances have constituted a significant part of total deposits of commercial banks, amounting to 7 per cent at the end of 1954. Yet they have grown less rapidly than total deposits, and their decreased importance is apparent among banks in each major category. Nonmember banks and member banks of each reserve classification have carried lower balances due from banks in relation to their own deposit liabilities.

Correspondent balances tend to fall into a pattern of interconnected clusters, with smaller banks carrying their major accounts in nearby cities and city banks carrying balances in other larger centers, especially New York City and often Chicago. Interbank deposits at the New York banks tend to move with changes in balances owned by reserve city member banks, and interbank deposits at reserve city banks tend to vary with nonmember and country member bank balances due from banks.

In connection with bankers' balances, the relative importance of various classes of banks has shifted markedly. New York central reserve city banks, whose interbank deposits amounted to 26 per cent of those for all insured commercial banks at the end of 1954, still play a major role. Yet their predominance has decreased as reserve city banks throughout the country have grown in importance as depositaries for other banks and as Chicago banks have maintained their position. Country member and nonmember commercial banks, which have grown especially rapidly during the period under study, have continued to maintain higher balances in proportion to their deposit liabilities than have other classes of banks. Thus, their holdings constitute three-fourths of total balances due from domestic banks. Since nonmember and country member banks tend to carry their acounts in reserve city banks, the interbank deposit liabilities of reserve city banks have come to exceed those of New York City. These changes reflect the general dispersion of industry together with increased agricultural incomes during this period.

Although there has been a movement of domestic bankers' balances away from New York City and toward a wider distribution through the country, interbank deposits are concentrated within larger banks located in the larger centers of population since these are the institutions which can normally render correspondent services most satisfactorily. In contrast to deposits due to banks, balances due from banks vary inversely with size of bank and center.

The geographical shifts of interbank balances have been sharp. The portion of all interbank deposits held in those Federal Reserve districts which include the

New England and Middle Atlantic states declined from about one-half in 1934 to one-third in 1954, and the portion dropped more for interbank deposits than for total deposits. The South, Southwest, and Central regions were increasingly important in both due to and due from banks. From 1934 to 1954, interbank deposits and balances due from banks generally followed changes in total deposits, although at a slower rate, and the growth in total deposits corresponded to changes in regional income.

The redistribution of bankers' balances has been toward those areas in which balances are large relative to total deposits. These are the Dallas, Kansas City, Atlanta, St. Louis, and Richmond Federal Reserve districts. The relatively high balances due from banks there and in the Minneapolis district are partially explained by their banking structure. They are regions of large numbers of commercial banks, especially small and nonmember banks. They contain all those banks which are not on the Federal Reserve par list. Except for the Richmond district, branch banking is little developed. Additional factors contributing to the importance of bankers' balances in these areas are the seasonal variation of deposits and of credit needs, reflecting agricultural activity, and the nationwide connections of their mineral and manufacturing production.

3. *Movements of Interbank Deposits*

Reflecting changes in total reserves of the banking system, variations in the demand for credit, and movements of funds within the economy, the fluctuations of interbank deposits fall into three periods. Rapid expansion of bankers' balances from 1934 to 1940 was followed by growth at a slower pace in the years from 1941 to 1945 and by a slight decline and then gradual recovery of previous levels from 1946 to 1954. In addition, variations occurred in response to recurring seasonal forces and to the alteration of the level of reserve requirements by the Board of Governors of the Federal Reserve System. These will be considered separately.

1934 TO 1940

From 1934 to the end of 1940 interbank deposits showed a strong upward surge, except for a sharp dip in 1937 (see Figure 1). Growth accompanied the inflow of funds from abroad and the easy credit conditions of most of the period.

Total reserves of member banks were increasing rapidly and fairly steadily throughout the period, chiefly as a result of international movements of funds. The $11.3 billion expansion of reserves was dominated by changes in the monetary gold stock and in foreign balances at Federal Reserve banks, which supplied $16.8

billion of reserves (Table 14). Although revaluation in 1934 together with domestic gold production accounts for $3.8 billion of the rise in the gold stock, gold imports were the chief source of the increase. The continued inflow of gold reflected a net merchandise export balance in part, but more largely the capital movements which resulted from political, financial, and economic uncertainty abroad and fear of war. After the outbreak of hostilities in Europe during 1939, foreign purchases of goods and services brought gold into the United States in large amount.

TABLE 14. CHANGES IN MEMBER BANK RESERVES WITH RELATED FACTORS
End of December, 1933 to 1940
(in millions of dollars)

Principal factors affecting reserves	
Gold and foreign account transactions	+ 16,830
Money in circulation	− 3,213
Treasury factors	− 1,510
Federal Reserve factors	− 809
Total	+ 11,297
Total reserves	+ 11,297
Required reserves	+ 5,541
Excess reserves	+ 5,756

Source: Computed from data in the 1954 *Annual Report* of the Board of Governors of the Federal Reserve System, pp. 74–75. Effects of the revaluation of gold are included in the figures for the gold stock and for Treasury factors. Figures do not add to total because of rounding.

The increase in total reserves was not accompanied by a proportionate expansion of required reserves, and therefore excess reserves accumulated rapidly. Through much of this period private credit demands were low, and the level of member bank loans remained below that of the 1920's. Although total loans and investments and total deposits expanded, they grew more slowly than did the dollar amount of reserves. Therefore, and in spite of the raising of reserve requirements by the Board of Governors, required reserves rose by only $5.5 billion and, consequently, excess reserves increased by $5.8 billion.

The impact of gold imports was felt first by the New York banks. In the early part of the period, reserves were fairly quickly disseminated through the country as commercial, industrial, financial, and governmental transactions took place. An especially important factor was the excess of Treasury receipts over disbursements in the New York area.[1] After war broke out in Europe, heavy purchases of goods and materials by foreign countries operated to spread the reserves throughout the country.

As aggregate excess reserves rose, individual banks could either allow their deposits with Federal Reserve banks to increase or use excess reserves to build up their correspondent balances. In so far as they chose to augment interbank accounts, excess reserves were redistributed within the banking system toward institutions which were conducting a large correspondent business.

Both reserve city and country member banks increased their balances due from banks, in amounts of $1.8 and $2.2 billion respectively (Table 15). Country banks' balances expanded by a larger amount than excess reserves and, relative to deposit liabilities, rose more than balances owned by reserve city banks. Insured nonmember commercial banks likewise increased their interbank balances (some of which constituted their legal reserves). Thus did the several classes of banks augment the reserves of their city correspondents.

---

[1] *Federal Reserve Bulletin,* January, 1937, pp. 2–3; September, 1939, p. 711.

TABLE 15. BALANCES WITH DOMESTIC BANKS IN AMOUNT AND AS PER CENT OF TOTAL DEPOSITS BY CLASS OF INSURED COMMERCIAL BANK

End of December, 1933 and 1940

	Amount (millions of dollars)			*Per Cent of Total Deposits*	
Class of Bank	*1933*	*1940*	*Change*	*1933*	*1940*
All member banks	2,031	6,185	+4,154	7	11
Country	769	3,002	+2,233	9	20
Reserve city	969	2,741	+1,772	10	14
Chicago	200	319	+ 119	12	9
New York City	93	122	+ 29	1	1
Nonmember, insured		2,019			29
All insured commercial		8,204			13

Source: *Banking and Monetary Statistics.* Percentages were computed.

Heavy net movement of interbank funds occurred. Net balances owned by country members rose by $1.8 billion (Table 16), and, from the end of 1934 to the end of 1940, net balances belonging to insured nonmember commercial banks increased by almost $1 billion.

TABLE 16. CHANGES IN EXCESS RESERVES AND IN NET DUE TO OR DUE FROM BANKS

All Member Banks by Reserve Classification

1934 to 1940

(millions of dollars)

Class of Bank	*Excess Reserves*	*Net Due to Banks*	*Net Due from Banks*
Central reserve city			
New York City	+3,248	+2,802	
Chicago	+ 267	+ 608	
Reserve city	+1,582	+ 766	
Country	+ 598		+1,834

Source: Computed from *Banking and Monetary Statistics.* Data on excess reserves relate to the monthly average of daily figures for January, 1934, and December, 1940. Net due to or from banks refers to the difference between interbank deposit liabilities and balances due from banks at the end of 1933 and 1940; both demand and time accounts are included, but not foreign balances.

The net inflow of interbank funds accounted for a large part of the increase in the excess reserves of New York City banks and for half the rise of excess reserves of reserve city member banks. For Chicago banks, the inflow of interbank deposits greatly exceeded the expansion of excess reserves over the period. Consequently, interbank deposits proved to be an important factor affecting the distribution of reserves during this period.

1941 to 1945

Bankers' balances grew more slowly than in the preceding period, since bank credit expanded greatly to finance wartime expenditures and idle funds largely disappeared. Interbank deposits at all insured commercial banks increased from $9.7 billion to $12.6 billion,[2] with most of the increase occurring after June, 1944 (see Figure 1).

These years were dominated by defense and war activity and finance. Bank credit rose swiftly, chiefly as a result of bank investment in government obligations and in small part as a result of loan expansion. Investments of insured commercial banks increased by $71.9 billion, almost all of which consisted of Treasury obligations, while loans rose by $7.4 billion.

Although bank credit was rising rapidly, total reserves of member banks expanded relatively little. The chief factors influencing reserves were Federal Reserve purchases of Treasury obligations, which supplied $22.1 billion, and an increase in the volume of money in circulation, which tended to absorb $19.8 billion (Table 17). Changes in the monetary gold stock and in foreign accounts at Federal Reserve banks were a third and much less important factor which, in sharp contrast

---

2 Beginning June 30, 1942, reciprocal bank balances are excluded. These amounted to $614 million on that date.

with preceding years, operated to decrease reserves by $1.7 billion. Gold movements reflected the low level of foreign reserves after the sustained losses in previous years together with the provision of American goods through our lend-lease program, the purchase by the United States of materials in other countries, and expenditures for our troops abroad.

TABLE 17. CHANGES IN MEMBER BANK RESERVES WITH RELATED FACTORS
End of December, 1940 to 1945
(millions of dollars)

Principal factors affecting reserves	
Federal Reserve holdings of government securities	+22,078
Money in circulation	−19,783
Gold and foreign account transactions	− 1,659
Treasury factors	+ 569
Federal Reserve discounts and advances	+ 246
Other Federal Reserve factors	+ 434
Total	+ 1,889
Total reserves	+ 1,889
Required reserves	+ 7,046
Excess reserves	− 5,157

Source: Computed from data in the 1954 *Annual Report* of the Board of Governors of the Federal Reserve System, pp. 74–75. Figures do not add to total because of rounding.

As a result of all factors, total reserves increased only $1.9 billion while required reserves rose $7 billion. Consequently, excess reserves fell sharply from a daily average of $6.8 billion in January, 1941, to about $1 billion late in 1943, and they fluctuated around this level through 1945.

The location and level of interbank balances and of excess reserves were affected by the variation in the pace of expansion in different classes of banks and by Treasury transactions. Growth of deposits was least rapid, about 70 to 90 per cent, in central reserve city banks.

Largely because of Treasury operations, deposits in these banks, especially those in New York City, increased less than their loans and investments. Treasury borrowing and tax receipts exceeded disbursements in the money centers. Banks in the South and West and in smaller cities tended to gain relative to the Northeast and the largest centers, reflecting expansion and high activity of war industries in the South and West, prosperity of agriculture, and location of training centers for the armed forces.

These changes brought a reduction of correspondent balances in New York City while banks in Chicago and reserve cities gained (Table 18). New York banks lost almost $800 million of funds through their correspondent accounts in 1941 and 1942, and they had regained only a part of the loss by the end of 1945. Such withdrawals by correspondents increased the difficulty of the New York banks in maintaining their reserve position; excess reserves fell toward zero, and borrowing from the Federal Reserve Bank was necessary. From the middle of 1944 through 1945 such borrowing generally exceeded excess reserves for New York banks as a group. Excess reserves of the Chicago banks also were largely eliminated in spite of their gain of funds through bankers' balances.

Reserve city banks, likewise, expanded nearly to the limit of their reserves. Excess reserves almost disappeared, dropping from an average of $2,016 million in January, 1941, to $300 or $400 million during most of 1945. Frequent borrowing occurred and free reserves (excess reserves minus borrowings at Federal Reserve banks) fluctuated around a low level during 1945.

In their effort to keep fully invested, reserve city

TABLE 18. GAIN AND LOSS OF FUNDS THROUGH INTERBANK BALANCES BY CLASS OF INSURED COMMERCIAL BANK

1941 to 1945 (millions of dollars)

Class of Bank	*Balances* [a]			*Balances* [b]			*Gain or Loss of Funds 1941–45*
	Dec. 31, 1940	*Dec. 31, 1942*	*Change*	*Dec. 31, 1942*	*Dec. 31, 1945*	*Change*	
New York City central reserve city member							
Due to banks	4,032	3,252	− 780	3,209	3,535	+ 326	
Due from banks	122	126	+ 4	82	78	− 4	
Net gain or loss							− 453
Chicago central reserve city member							
Due to banks	997	1,138	+ 141	1,105	1,292	+ 187	
Due from banks	319	196	− 123	164	200	+ 36	
Net gain or loss							+ 415
Reserve city member							
Due to banks	3,919	5,207	+ 1,288	4,831	6,307	+ 1,476	
Due from banks	2,741	2,578	− 163	2,202	2,174	− 28	
Net gain or loss							+ 2,955
Country member							
Due to banks	633	1,017	+ 384	957	1,199	+ 242	
Due from banks	3,002	3,759	+ 757	3,699	4,665	+ 966	
Net gain or loss							− 1,097
Nonmember, insured							
Due to banks	95	145	+ 50	133	233	+ 100	
Due from banks	2,019	2,946	+ 927	2,934	3,959	+ 1,025	
Net gain or loss							− 1,802

Source: *Banking and Monetary Statistics*, *Federal Reserve Bulletin*, and *Member Bank Call Report* for December 31, 1942. "Due to banks" refers to demand deposits only. Foreign balances are excluded.

[a] Reciprocal balances are not excluded. For comparability with 1940, the 1942 figures were adjusted by adding reciprocal balances. On December 31, 1942, these amounted to $43 million at New York City banks, $33 million at Chicago banks, $377 million at reserve city banks, $60 million at country banks, and $12 million at insured nonmember commercial banks, as reported in the *Member Bank Call Report* and the *Federal Reserve Bulletin*.

[b] Reciprocal balances are excluded.

banks somewhat reduced their holdings of amounts due from other banks. Balances fell sharply from $2.8 billion in June of 1941 to $1.8 billion [8] at the end of 1943 and then rose in the following two years to $2.2 billion (see Figure 3). Two billion dollars appeared to constitute a kind of minimum working balance for the reserve city banks. In relation to demand deposits adjusted, balances due from banks dropped from 29 per cent at the beginning of 1941 to about 10 per cent in 1943–45.

Although they drew down their own correspondent balances only slightly, reserve city banks gained heavily as receivers of deposits from other banks. Thus through movements of correspondent accounts, their net gain of funds during the period amounted to almost $3 billion (Table 18).

Excess reserves at country member banks declined slightly from the beginning of the period but fluctuated rather widely. Nevertheless, their balances due from banks expanded by $1.7 billion, rising rapidly from $3.0 to $4.7 billion (Table 18). Likewise, insured nonmember banks increased their interbank balances (including legal reserves) from $2.0 to $4.0 billion. Consequently, the net loss of funds through interbank transactions amounted to approximately $3 billion for these two classes of banks during this period.

Although they increased their holdings of amounts due from banks, country member and insured nonmember banks did not add to these balances as rapidly as their own deposit liabilities expanded. At country members, due from banks dropped from 38 to 20 per

[8] These data are not strictly comparable, since reciprocal balances are not excluded prior to June 30, 1942, at which time they amounted to $428 million.

cent of demand deposits adjusted during the period, and at insured nonmember banks there was a similar drop, from 60 to 38 per cent.

Several factors explain the behavior of country member and nonmember banks in expanding balances with other banks and maintaining excess reserves while balances owned by reserve city and central reserve city banks showed little or no expansion and their excess reserves disappeared for the most part. First of all, it

TABLE 19. CHANGES IN TOTAL LOANS AND INVESTMENTS AND HOLDINGS OF TREASURY OBLIGATIONS BY CLASS OF INSURED COMMERCIAL BANK
1941 to 1945 (amounts in billions of dollars)

	Total Loans and Investments				*United States Treasury Obligations*		
			Increase				
Class of Bank	*Dec. 31, 1940*	*Dec. 31, 1945*	*Amount*	*Per Cent*	*Dec. 31, 1940*	*Dec. 31, 1945*	*Amount of Increase*
Central reserve city member							
New York City	$10.9	$26.1	$15.2	140	$6.0	$17.6	$11.5
Chicago	2.4	5.9	3.6	150	1.3	4.2	2.9
Reserve city member	13.0	40.1	27.1	208	5.2	29.6	24.3
Country member	10.8	35.0	24.2	223	3.3	27.0	23.7
Nonmember, insured	5.4	14.6	9.2	170	1.2	10.6	9.3

Source: *Federal Reserve Bulletin.* Increases were computed.

is clear that balances did not accumulate because of a failure of smaller banks to expand. The $24 billion increase in total loans and investments of country member banks was almost as large in dollar amount as the $27 billion rise at reserve city banks, and the percentage increase was higher (Table 19). The increase consisted almost entirely of holdings of United States government obligations, since the expansion of loans was limited by the degree to which the Treasury itself financed wartime expansion through progress payments and other means and by anti-inflationary policies which restricted certain types of credit (such as consumer credit through Regulation W) and discouraged bank lending to finance customer purchases of government bonds.

Country banks expanded their holdings of government obligations greatly but not to the extent of eliminating excess reserves and drawing down correspondent balances. This was in the face of Federal Reserve policy to maintain the existing structure of rates on Treasury obligations and so to stabilize the government security market and in the face of Federal Reserve policy to purchase Treasury bills on a fixed discount basis. During the war years Treasury bills were made highly liquid by the willingness of Federal Reserve banks to buy all bills offered at a fixed discount of .375 per cent, with repurchase option. Purchase could be for immediate credit and repurchase with immediate delivery so that bills were very nearly equivalent to cash.[4]

Smaller banks, whether member or nonmember, did not push their investments further for several reasons. Balances due from banks had been higher relative to total deposit liabilities and to demand deposits adjusted in the 1930's than in preceding years, but the higher ratio had existed for some time and perhaps a higher ratio had come to be accepted as more or less normal and desirable for working purposes. Consequently the decline in the ratio of balances to deposit liabilities was retarded during the war years, and balances continued to rise in dollar amount.

Other reasons for not expanding investments further to the point of squeezing out excess reserves and of re-

---

4 According to policy actions of the Federal Reserve Open Market Committee taken from April to September, 1942.

ducing balances with banks are suggested in Congressional hearings on the absorption of exchange charges by correspondent banks in late 1943 and early 1944.[5] Lack of familiarity with techniques, especially the Treasury bill purchase plan, was one. Another reason given was the expectation that the close of hostilities would bring deposit withdrawals and increased demand for loans.

The low rate of return possible, especially on short-term obligations, was another factor in the failure to expand investments further. The attitude toward low yields on short-term Treasury obligations is suggested by the remark of one bank officer, president of two small banks, before the House Committee: "I have not bought any of this one-fourth-of-1-percent stuff," although he had invested in short-term government bonds.[6] The low yield on short-term Treasury obligations may well have appeared less attractive to officers of smaller banks than to those of larger institutions, since interest rates on loans of smaller banks tend to be considerably higher than those at larger banks (chiefly because of the size and nature of the loans).[7] Thus by comparison with past use of funds, returns of .375 or .875 per cent seemed relatively less attractive to the management of smaller banks.

Hesitation to reduce interbank balances or to draw down excess reserves further was reinforced by the very rapid expansion of large training centers for the armed

---

5 Congress of the United States, House of Representatives, Committee on Banking and Currency, 78th Cong., 2d Sess., *Hearings on H.R. 3956, Absorption of Exchange Charges,* December, 1943, and January and February, 1944, esp. pp. 266–72 and 294.

6 *Ibid.,* p. 294.

7 Richard Youngdahl, "The Structure of Interest Rates on Business Loans at Member Banks," *Federal Reserve Bulletin,* July, 1947, p. 809.

services and the installation of war plants in smaller centers. Their needs for payroll currency and check cashing facilities placed heavy cash demands upon small banks, which maintained their liquidity by large interbank deposits in nearby centers.

Implicit in much of the discussion in the Congressional hearings in 1943–44 was the belief that interbank balances were enlarged by the practice of correspondents' absorbing exchange charges arising out of remittance at less than par. This practice, in which some, but not all, banks engaged, affected the location of interbank deposits but not their aggregate volume. If absorption had been an important determinant of the total volume of bankers' balances, a reduction of balances would have followed the restriction of absorption.[8] This was not the case. Balances continued to rise while the ruling was under discussion in 1943 and 1944 and after some banks had ceased to absorb exchange, and they rose further in 1945, well after the compliance date. (Since the New York banks did not absorb exchange,[9] the drop in interbank deposits in New York City during 1943 resulted from other factors.)

Within this period sharp movements of bankers' balances were caused by war loan drives. From April, 1943, to June 30, 1947, war loan deposits (balances to the credit of the Treasury arising from subscriptions

---

[8] The ruling of the Board of Governors restricting absorption of exchange charges was under discussion in 1936 and 1937, but not until August, 1943, was an opinion announced, in a specific case, that absorption constituted payment of interest and was, therefore, illegal. After Congressional hearings and public discussion, the Board in June, 1945, requested general compliance of member banks by August 1, 1945.

[9] Congress of the United States, House of Representatives, Committee on Banking and Currency, 78th Cong., 2d Sess., *Hearings on H.R. 3956, Absorption of Exchange Charges,* December, 1943, and January and February, 1944, p. 38.

to government securities) in member banks were exempt from reserve requirements. Consequently, war loan drives brought a temporary lowering of the dollar amount of required reserves as funds were transferred from nongovernmental to war loan accounts in payment for subscriptions. As the Treasury disbursed its funds, other deposits in commercial banks rose with a consequent increase of required reserves. Both country and reserve city member banks allowed their balances with other banks to increase as reserves were temporarily freed by bond drives. Thus interbank balances on the December call date in 1944 and 1945 were enlarged by the Treasury loan drives occurring at those times. Such movements were short-term fluctuations, somewhat similar to those that take place on tax and interest payment dates and during Treasury refunding operations, all of which are likely to bring heavy movements of bankers' balances, especially those in New York City.

1946 TO 1954

After an initial decline, interbank deposits appear to have reached a minimum level of generally convenient working balances during these postwar years, for they were maintained at a fairly constant percentage of demand deposits adjusted. Demand for bank credit was active in most categories of loans—commercial and industrial loans, real estate loans, and consumer credit, a relatively new field for commercial banks as a whole. Interest rates were generally higher. Thus funds could be, and were, actively invested and interbank balances did not accumulate.

Deposits due to banks were generally somewhat lower in dollar amount from 1946 into 1949, and thereafter they gradually increased. End of year data for insured commercial banks showed a drop in interbank deposits from $12.6 billion at the end of 1945 to $10.3 billion in 1948, followed by a rise to $13.4 billion in 1954.

In the year 1946, balances owned by insured commercial banks dropped by $1.6 billion, of which $1.3 billion was attributable to country member and insured nonmember banks. Balances were drawn down as commercial banks as a whole suffered a drain of reserves through the Treasury debt retirement program. In addition, loans to business expanded throughout the banking system and bank funds were needed to meet loan demands. Largely because of the drop in security loans at city banks following the Victory Loan campaign at the end of 1945, country member and insured nonmember banks showed the highest rate of increase of total loans and thus felt pressed to reduce their correspondent balances.

From 1946 to 1954, interbank deposits of each class of bank were maintained in quite stable relationship to other deposits (Table 20). This is in contrast to experience during the Second World War, when the ratios of bankers' balances fell sharply from their 1941 level. In 1946 interbank balances apparently had reached a minimum for working purposes, and thereafter the ratios showed little variation from year to year in each class of bank. Although ratios varied widely for member banks of different reserve classification and for nonmember banks, the ratio of interbank to total deposit liabilities and of balances due from banks to demand deposits adjusted fluctuated within a relatively narrow range for each group of banks on either June or December call dates.

Interbank deposits did little by way of redistributing the reserves of the banking system as a whole during this period (Table 21). Reserve city banks gained less than

$500 million of funds through movements of interbank balances while other classes of banks gained or lost only small amounts. Shifting of funds because of the

TABLE 20. DEMAND DEPOSITS DUE TO DOMESTIC BANKS AS PER CENT OF TOTAL DEPOSITS AND BALANCES DUE FROM DOMESTIC BANKS AS PER CENT OF DEMAND DEPOSITS ADJUSTED

Range of Ratios for All Insured Commercial Banks by Class
December Call Dates, 1941–45 and 1946–54

	Interbank Deposits as Per Cent of Total Deposits		*Balances Due from Domestic Banks as Per Cent of Demand Deposits Adjusted*	
Class of Bank	*1941–45*	*1946–54*	*1941–45*	*1946–54*
New York City central reserve city member				
maximum	20	13	[a]	[a]
minimum	12	12	[a]	[a]
Chicago central reserve city member				
maximum	25	19	13	5
minimum	18	16	5	3
Reserve city member				
maximum	19	12	23	8
minimum	13	11	9	7
Country member				
maximum	5	2	33	15
minimum	3	2	20	13
Nonmember, insured				
maximum	1	2	57	30
minimum	1	1	38	27
All insured				
maximum	14	8	23	12
minimum	9	7	14	11

Sources: *Banking and Monetary Statistics, Member Bank Call Reports, Federal Reserve Bulletin,* and unpublished data of the Board of Governors.

[a] Ratios less than 1 per cent, except in 1941.

movement of correspondent accounts was less than that which occurred during the years of the Second World War and markedly less than in the prewar years.

Business depression and a low level of economic activity may contribute to an expansion of bankers' balances, as in the 1930's, but the two recessions in the postwar years brought no such clear response. Monthly

TABLE 21. GAIN AND LOSS OF FUNDS THROUGH INTERBANK BALANCES BY CLASS OF INSURED COMMERCIAL BANK
1946 to 1954
(millions of dollars)

Class of Bank	*Amount* *Dec. 31, 1945*	*Dec. 31, 1954*	*Change*	*Gain or Loss of Funds*
New York City central reserve city member				
Due to banks	3,535	3,336	− 199	
Due from banks	78	67	− 11	
Net gain or loss				− 188
Chicago central reserve city member				
Due to banks	1,292	1,264	− 28	
Due from banks	200	162	− 38	
Net gain or loss				+ 10
Reserve city member				
Due to banks	6,307	6,946	+ 639	
Due from banks	2,174	2,327	+ 153	
Net gain or loss				+ 486
Country member				
Due to banks	1,199	1,469	+ 270	
Due from banks	4,665	5,057	+ 392	
Net gain or loss				− 122
Nonmember, insured				
Due to banks	233	377	+ 144	
Due from banks	3,959	4,243	+ 284	
Net gain or loss				− 140

Source: *Federal Reserve Bulletin* and unpublished data of the Federal Reserve Board. "Due to banks" refers to demand deposits due to domestic banks. "Due from banks" includes all balances due from domestic banks.

averages of balances due to and due from banks did not increase early in 1949, when economic activity declined. Not until reserve requirements were changed did some expansion of balances occur. This was a relatively short drop in general business activity, however, with recovery beginning in the second half of 1949.

In the second downturn of the economy, beginning in 1953 and continuing into 1954, interbank balances increased in dollar amount but not in relation to total deposits. The expansion also reflected the reduction of reserve requirements by the Board of Governors. The failure of interbank balances to increase strongly during the downturn of 1953–54 is largely explained by the tight reserve position of banks as a whole. Member banks had found it necessary to borrow from Federal Reserve banks late in 1952 and in 1953 and, except for country banks, borrowings tended to exceed excess reserves. Hence the easing of credit demand made it possible for the banks to reduce their own borrowing and to maintain free reserves once again, but there was little opportunity to expand balances with other banks.

In summary, the movements of bankers' balances were affected by widely differing influences during the three periods. From 1934 to 1940, interbank deposits at member banks expanded rapidly in dollar amount from $3.1 to $9.6 billion and they rose from 12 to 17 per cent of total deposits. The expansion was caused basically by the inflow of gold. The resulting increase in reserves for the banking system as a whole came at a time when large additional reserves could not be profitably and satisfactorily put to work by the banks. Excess reserves therefore accumulated. Through interbank deposits the location of excess reserves within the banking system was shifted markedly, especially toward banks in New York City.

In the war and postwar years, interbank balances grew much more slowly than during the 1930's. Relatively little increase occurred in total reserves and the expansion of bank credit, together with a larger volume of money in circulation, caused the virtual disappearance of excess reserves. Opportunity for the use of bank funds through investment in Treasury obligations during the war and through loans to private borrowers and investment in government securities after the end of the war has meant that interbank balances have grown slowly in dollar amount and their size has declined relative to other deposits.

Country member and insured nonmember commercial banks grew very rapidly during the war years because of decentralization of industrial and military activity and because of increased prosperity of agriculture, and their growth extended into later years. They continued to maintain correspondent balances at a level high relative to their own deposit liabilities. This reflected both their need for the services of the city correspondent and their reluctance and inability to take full advantage of the high liquidity of government securities by pushing investments to the maximum permitted by their reserves. Banks in reserve cities grew almost as rapidly as country members and nonmembers. In contrast, they were able to utilize their funds more fully and thus their balances due from banks became relatively less important. Reduction by reserve city banks of their holdings of deposits with other banks partially explains the decline of bankers' balances at New York City banks and, furthermore, reserve city banks were the chief recipients of increased funds from country member and nonmember banks.

SEASONAL MOVEMENT

Interbank balances reveal a fairly regular seasonal pattern with a downswing in the early months of the year to a low point in May and then a general upswing. However, the pattern varies with the class of bank. Indexes of seasonal variation for member banks by reserve classification, which were derived from monthly averages of daily figures from January, 1946, to June, 1955, are shown in Figures 8 and 9.[10]

The strongest seasonal element appeared in country bank balances due from banks and in interbank deposit liabilities of reserve city banks (Figure 8). Fluctuations of these two series are closely similar in direct-tion and magnitude, falling each month from January through May and rising through November. In December, country bank balances typically drop slightly while interbank deposits of reserve city banks remain unchanged. The U-shaped pattern of country bank balances reflects the general downturn of gross demand deposits in the early months of the year as farm income drops sharply and the upswing of deposits as farm receipts rise sharply in August, September, and October. Likewise wholesale and retail trade are generally low in the first part of the year and higher in later months, and industrial production normally reaches its peak in the fall.

Similarity of seasonal pattern also appears between reserve city bank balances due from banks and New York City interbank deposits (Figure 8). As did the preceding series, these move generally downward from

---

[10] Indexes were computed by the method of ratios to twelve-month moving averages. Data begin with January, 1946, except for New York City interbank deposits, which begin with July, 1946.

Interbank data refer to demand balances due from domestic banks and to interbank demand deposit liabilities. At Chicago and reserve city banks, deposits due to foreign banks are included. For New York banks, deposits due to domestic banks have been estimated by use of data of amounts due to foreign banks at weekly reporting member banks in New York City.

January to May and upward thereafter, but the over-all amplitude is smaller and the downswing and upswing less continuous. Narrower seasonal movements result from the diversity of business and financial transactions affecting these banks. Interbank deposits, especially those in New York City, have been considerably affected

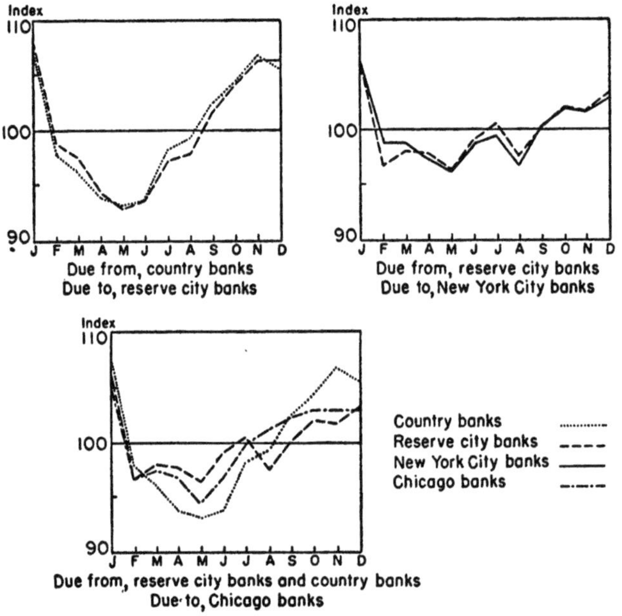

FIGURE 8. INDEX OF SEASONAL VARIATION OF BALANCES DUE TO AND DUE FROM OTHER BANKS
All Member Banks by Reserve Classification

Source: Computed from monthly averages of daily figures, January, 1946, through June, 1955, as published in the *Federal Reserve Bulletin.* "Due from" refers to demand balances due from domestic banks. "Due to" refers to demand deposits due to foreign and domestic banks in connection with reserve city and Chicago central reserve city banks. For New York City central reserve city banks, estimates of demand deposits due to domestic banks were obtained by using monthly averages of deposits due to foreign banks at banks reporting weekly, and for this calculation data begin with July, 1946.

by tax payments, and by Treasury and corporate interest payments, with consequent accumulation of balances in March and in June and July and in September.

As with other classes of banks, interbank deposits at Chicago banks move generally downward to May and then upward. Their pattern is not clearly similar to

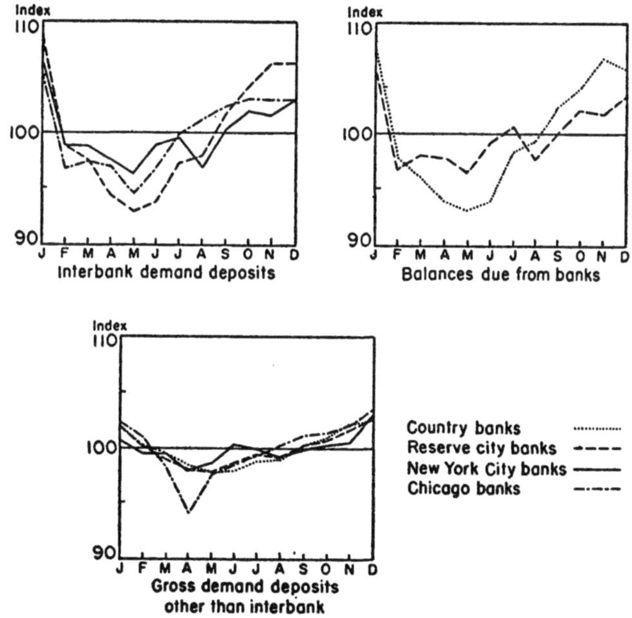

FIGURE 9. INDEX OF SEASONAL VARIATION OF BALANCES DUE TO AND DUE FROM OTHER BANKS AND GROSS DEMAND DEPOSITS OTHER THAN INTERBANK
All Member Banks by Reserve Classification
Source: See Figure 8.

the pattern of balances due from banks owned by either reserve city or country banks but appears to be a mixture of the two elements (Figure 8).

The relationships between classes of banks suggested by similarity of seasonal patterns are borne out by divergences of movements. While a general horseshoe shape appears in each, interbank deposits at the several classes of banks do differ (Figure 9), and country bank balances vary from those of reserve city banks.

The seasonal behavior of interbank balances confirms the earlier statement that smaller banks tend to hold their major accounts at regional correspondents and that interbank deposits in New York are largely owned by reserve city banks. Chicago appears to be midway, and influences of neither country nor reserve city banks predominate.

Relative to their size, interbank balances vary more widely from one season to another than do gross demand deposits other than interbank deposits (Figure 9). On the whole and for each class of bank except Chicago, interbank balances show wider variation. The sharp drop in other deposits at the Chicago banks in April reflects depositors' movement of funds out of Chicago in preparation for the April first property tax assessment there.

Since correspondent banks are heavily used in the clearing of checks, transfer of funds, making of payments on securities and other transactions, the seasonal pattern of interbank balances has been compared with that of bank debits. Fluctuations of bank debits indicate variations in the volume of money payments of all kinds. Included are not only payments related to trade and production but also those connected with tax collections and with financial transactions, such as security purchases and interest payments. An earlier study found that seasonal variations in interbank balances did correlate positively with bank debits by Federal Reserve district.[11]

---

[11] Beckhart and Smith, *Sources and Movements of Funds*, pp. 266–68.

The seasonal behavior of interbank deposits in New York City shows similarity to that of bank debits there.[12] Although interbank deposits fluctuate much less widely than debits to demand deposit accounts, except inter-

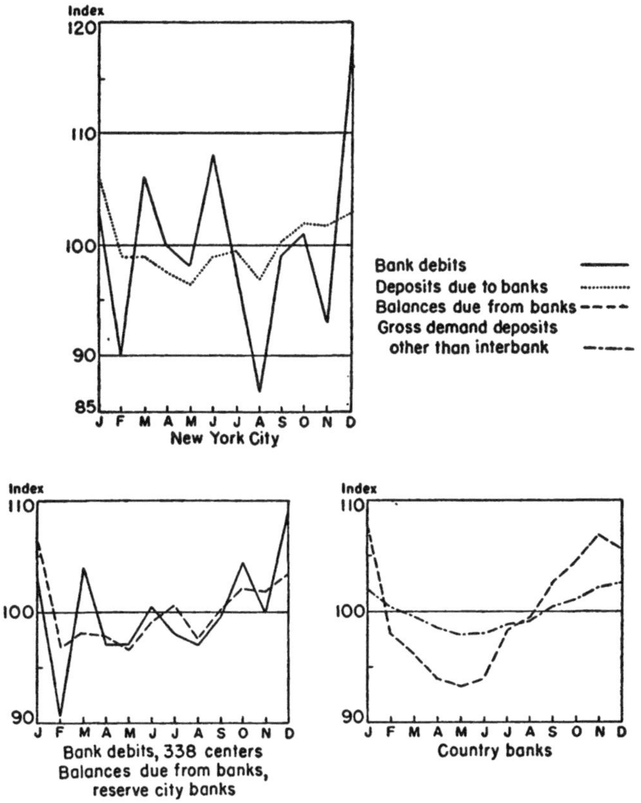

FIGURE 10. INDEX OF SEASONAL VARIATION OF BANK DEBITS AND INTERBANK BALANCES

Source: Bank debit factors are from the Federal Reserve Bank of New York and relate to debits to demand deposits (except interbank and United States government accounts). For New York City, 1952–54 factors were used. For 338 centers, 1950–54 factors were used. For sources of other data see Figure 8.

---

12 Seasonal adjustment factors are those compiled by the Federal Reserve Bank of New York.

bank and United States government accounts, the due to banks generally moves in the same direction (Figure 10). Bank debits for 338 centers [13] are related in similar fashion to reserve city banks' balances due from banks (Figure 10). This reflects the relationship between the flow of local activity and the need for funds in New York City, Chicago, or elsewhere.

Country bank balances, on the other hand, bear little resemblance to the bank debits series, although regional comparisons might reveal such relationship. At country member banks as a whole, the seasonal movement of balances follows the U-shaped pattern of gross demand deposits other than interbank, but in exaggerated degree (Figure 10). This behavior, which contrasts with that of reserve city banks, tends to bear out the suggestion made earlier that balances serve, in part, as a reservoir and that they are drawn down under the pressure of heavy credit demands in the spring when deposits fall and are built up when seasonal inflow of payments occurs.

RESPONSE TO CHANGES IN RESERVE REQUIREMENTS

The response of bankers' balances to changes in reserve requirements by the Board of Governors of the Federal Reserve System has been examined since the movement of interbank funds affects the distribution of reserves within the banking system and may have some effect upon the volume of required reserves. Pronounced response could lessen the predictability of monetary controls by shifting the location of their impact.

---

[13] Centers other than New York City, Boston, Philadelphia, Chicago, Detroit, San Francisco, and Los Angeles.

Prior to the Second World War, reserve requirements were changed three times.[14] Increases were made in 1936 and 1937 and a decrease in 1938. Each of these affected interbank deposits, but the sharpest reaction occurred in 1937.

Requirements were increased by one-half in 1936, effective in August, and this involved a reduction of about $1.5 billion in total excess reserves.[15] In July and August, following the announcement of the change, between $100 and $200 million of bankers' balances were withdrawn from New York City and withdrawals were also made from banks in other cities.[16] Interbank balances were used in a small degree to adjust legal reserve positions.

In order to reduce further the potential expansion of credit upon the basis of existing excess reserves, the Board increased requirements by an additional one-third in 1937, announced in January and effective March 1 and May 1. The change in 1936 together with that of 1937 brought a doubling of requirements within less than nine months and raised them to their statutory maximum. The action in 1937 was expected to eliminate a further $1.5 billion of excess reserves.[17]

In response to the change, interbank deposits dipped sharply during the spring of 1937, dropping from $6.4 billion at the end of 1936 to $5.3 billion on June 30, 1937, a decline of $1.1 billion for all member banks.

---

14 Authority to change requirements was given to the Board in 1935 (after a grant on an emergency basis in 1933).

15 Board of Governors of the Federal Reserve System, *Annual Report*, 1936, p. 13.

16 *Federal Reserve Bulletin*, January, 1937, p. 5.

17 Board of Governors of the Federal Reserve System, *Annual Report*, 1937, p. 196.

Such withdrawal did not directly affect the total volume of reserves but it did affect the location of reserves and of excess reserves.

The brunt of withdrawals was felt by New York City banks. The net loss of $451 million through interbank accounts (Table 22) constituted an additional

TABLE 22. GAIN AND LOSS OF FUNDS THROUGH INTERBANK BALANCES
MEMBER BANKS BY RESERVE CLASSIFICATION
December 31, 1936, to June 30, 1937
(millions of dollars)

	Interbank Balances			
Class of Bank	*Dec. 31, 1936*	*June 30, 1937*	*Change*	*Gain or Loss of Funds*
New York City central reserve city				
Due to banks	2,493	2,014	−479	
Due from banks	133	105	− 28	
Net gain or loss				−451
Chicago central reserve city				
Due to banks	599	536	− 63	
Due from banks	188	156	− 32	
Net gain or loss				− 31
Reserve city				
Due to banks	2,826	2,339	−487	
Due from banks	1,816	1,392	−424	
Net gain or loss				− 63
Country				
Due to banks	483	409	− 74	
Due from banks	1,929	1,554	−375	
Net gain or loss				+301

Source: Computed from data in *Banking and Monetary Statistics.* "Due to banks" refers to demand deposits due to domestic banks. "Due from banks" refers to balances with domestic banks.

drain upon their reserves at a time when reserves were not much more than adequate to absorb the $600 million increase in required reserves resulting from Board action. Consequently the movement of bankers' balances made it more difficult for the New York banks to meet the increase in requirements and contributed to the necessity to reduce investment in Treasury obligations from $4.2 to $3.6 billion in the first six months of 1937. As a result of all factors involved, excess reserves dropped from $697 million in December, 1936, to $176 million in June, 1937.

Reserve city banks also suffered heavy withdrawals of $487 million of bankers' balances, but they were able as a group to counteract most of this loss by reducing their own balances with other banks by $424 million. Likewise in Chicago, half the drain of interbank deposits was offset by the reduction of balances due from banks. Consequently, Chicago and reserve city banks reduced their investments and allowed excess reserves to fall by proportionately smaller amounts than New York banks.

In contrast, country banks gained $301 million through interbank deposits. Therefore their excess reserves fell in smaller degree, from $498 million (December, 1936) to $341 million (June, 1937), and unlike other member banks they were able to expand total loans and investments.

Thus through the movement of bankers' balances the impact of the 1937 change in requirements was partially shifted. The distribution of reserves was altered and thereby the lending-investing ability of the several classes of banks was affected. Pressure on reserves was lessened at country member banks and augmented at city banks with especially heavy effect in New York City. Country member banks met a large part of their increased requirements by withdrawing correspondent balances, and total credit extended by country banks expanded with relatively little drop in excess reserves. At reserve city and Chicago banks, the effect of the increase in requirements was augmented by the loss of interbank deposits, which they in turn partially offset by reducing their own balances with other banks. Considerable pressure was placed upon New York banks by the drain of funds to out-of-town correspondents.

The events of 1937 reveal that interbank balances add an element of unpredictability in the exercise of general credit control by means of changes in reserve requirements. Reserves of New York City banks in December, 1936, were adequate to meet the 1937 increase in their requirements, which amounted to approximately $650 million. The Board of Governors estimated that all but 12 of the 37 central reserve city banks in New York had sufficient reserves (together with half their balances due from banks) to meet the higher requirements, and that only about $100 million of additional reserves were needed to supply the requirements of these 12 banks.[18] Yet existing excess reserves were not really available for meeting higher requirements because of the drain of $479 million through the withdrawal of correspondent balances. Other elements also affected the situation, such as Treasury financing which led to further pressure on New York banks. However, the movement of interbank balances greatly augmented the anticipated pressure upon New York City banks, augmented somewhat the pressure placed upon Chicago and reserve city banks, and at the same time diminished the pressure upon the reserve position of country member banks.

In 1938, after the severe drop in 1937, interbank deposits resumed their upward climb and by the end of the year were as high as they had been in 1936. Reserves were freed in April by a $750 million reduction

[18] Board of Governors of the Federal Reserve System, *Annual Report*, 1937, p. 4.

of requirements,[19] which contributed to the expansion of interbank deposits. From March to June country banks reduced their balances at Federal Reserve banks and allowed their correspondent accounts to rise about equally with excess reserves. Likewise reserve city bank balances due from banks expanded approximately the same amount as excess reserves. Thus the decrease in requirements contributed to a slight rise of interbank deposits. Subsequently the lower level of requirements, together with larger reserves for the banking system as a whole and the slackening of credit demands, led to rapid expansion of interbank deposits.

The next change in requirements was an increase in 1941, which absorbed an estimated $1.2 billion of reserves.[20] Losses of interbank deposits occurred at weekly reporting member banks at the end of October and early in November in reflection of this change, which became effective November 1. Member bank balances due from banks dropped between September 24 and December 31, with a decline of almost $300 million for reserve city banks and $77 million for country banks. Both groups allowed excess reserves to drop as well as correspondent balances.

During the war and early postwar years requirements were unchanged except for adjustments applying to central reserve city banks only, but in following years they were altered several times. The effects of these changes can be observed not only through weekly (Wednesday) figures of demand deposits due to domestic banks and call report data, but also through monthly

---

19 *Ibid.*, 1938, p. 27.
20 *Ibid.*, 1941, p. 7.

averages of daily figures for demand deposits due to[21] and due from banks.

In September, 1948, reserve requirements were increased for each class of member bank. This change of two percentage points in legal requirements against demand deposits and 1.5 per cent against time deposits involved an increase of $2 billion in required reserves, or approximately $700 million for country banks, $700 million for reserve city, $400 million for New York City and $100 million for Chicago banks.

The increase in reserve requirements was met in part by the use of interbank balances but also by the sale of government securities and by a reduction in excess reserves. Interbank deposits were drawn down substantially[22] when country banks were adjusting to the new requirements. Decreases occurred at reporting member banks in the weeks ending September 22 and September 29. For New York City banks the decline of deposits due to domestic banks amounted to $356 million and $147 million for the two weeks respectively, while banks outside New York City showed a drop of $553 million and $150 million. However, funds returned to the city correspondents within succeeding weeks as depositing banks sold government securities and placed the proceeds in interbank accounts.[23]

Such withdrawals were apparently sharp, temporary effects of the change in reserve requirements, but the

---

21 For banks outside New York City, monthly averages include amounts due to foreign as well as domestic banks, but the inclusion of foreign deposits has little effect. For New York City only, data have been adjusted to exclude amounts due to foreign banks by the use of averages of weekly reporting banks.

22 "Money Market in October," *Monthly Review* (Federal Reserve Bank of New York), November, 1948, p. 113.

23 *Ibid.*

continuing effect was to retard the usual seasonal upswing of interbank balances. Thus the monthly data (averages of daily figures) did not show the usual rise in the fall and winter months. Monthly averages adjusted for seasonal variation [24] show that balances owned by country banks were about $200 million lower in October than in the months preceding the change in requirements, and those owned by reserve city banks were about $100 million less.

The use of interbank deposits therefore placed added pressure upon the reserve position of city correspondents and eased the adjustment of country banks. As shown by monthly averages, city banks suffered chiefly in the failure of interbank deposits to make their customary upswing in the last quarter of the year. This was true for New York central reserve city banks. Average interbank deposits at Chicago banks dropped about $30 million from July, in contrast to the usual increase of about that amount late in the year. At reserve city banks, interbank deposits rose in September and October but after adjustment for the usual seasonal variation they showed a drop of $75 or $100 million. However, balances due from banks (adjusted) showed a corresponding decline and, consequently, movement of interbank balances had little net effect upon reserve city banks as a whole.

In 1949, reserves released by a series of reductions of requirements flowed chiefly into enlarged holdings of government obligations. An estimated total of $3.8 billion of reserves [25] was freed by these reductions,

---

24 The seasonal index discussed earlier in this chapter was used to remove the effect of the usual seasonal pattern from data of monthly averages of daily figures.

25 Board of Governors of the Federal Reserve System, *Annual Report,* 1949, p. 5.

which took effect from May 1 through September 1. With the release of $1.4 billion of reserves, country banks increased their due from banks by about $369 million (adjusted), or $660 million (unadjusted), from April to September. Excess reserves rose more than $200 million. However, the greatest effect upon country banks was in the expansion of their Treasury portfolios. Reserve city banks, for whom another $1.4 billion of reserves was freed, allowed fewer of their released funds to accumulate in other banks. From April to September, their balances rose only $41 million on an adjusted basis, or $79 million unadjusted.

It was chiefly the reserve city banks which acquired funds through bankers' balances, and this inflow amounted to $232 million, adjusted for seasonal variation, or $585 million unadjusted. New York and Chicago banks gained $154 million ($287 million unadjusted). Thus both reserve and central reserve city banks received funds through increases in interbank deposits. Reserve city banks gained somewhat more heavily, reflecting the fact that balances were augmented chiefly by country banks at their regional correspondent rather than by reserve city banks in New York or Chicago.

The development of inflationary pressures in 1950, especially after the outbreak of hostilities in Korea in June, led to an increase in reserve requirements as part of the Federal Reserve policy in restraint of credit. Announced in December and effective in steps from January 11 to February 1, 1951, this change was estimated to absorb $2 billion of reserves, with about $1.8 billion of the increase occurring in January.[26] Adjust-

[26] "Money Market in January," *Monthly Review* (Federal Reserve Bank of New York), February, 1951, p. 17.

ment to the initial change was made easier because of the supplying of reserves through large, routine money market transactions, especially Treasury operations and a seasonal return flow of currency, each of which increased member bank reserves about $700 million in the three weeks ending January 17.[27]

The largest change accompanying the increase in requirements was again in holdings of government securities. New York central reserve city banks and reserve city banks reduced their investment in Treasury obligations by $884 million and $1,359 million respectively in January and February as changes in requirements took place and as total loans increased.

Substantial withdrawals by their correspondents made the adjustment of banks in New York and other leading cities more difficult. In the four weeks from January 3 to January 31, interbank deposits dropped $593 million at weekly reporting member banks in New York City and $1,539 million in other leading cities. Thus interbank balances were used heavily by correspondent banks in making their own short-time adjustments.

Averages of daily figures, however, do not reveal large scale shifting of bankers' balances from month to month. At both reserve city and central reserve city banks, interbank deposits usually show a seasonal increase in January and downswing in February. In 1951 the rise in January was less and the drop in February somewhat greater than usual. Therefore, on an adjusted basis, deposits declined by small amounts in January and February: $65 million and $7 million at New York City banks, $8 million and $15 million at Chicago banks, and $18 million and $73 million at reserve city banks. The loss of deposits by reserve city banks was

---

27 *Ibid.*

partially offset by a drop of $63 million in balances due from banks (adjusted) during these two months, and the net loss of funds for these banks as a group amounted to only $28 million for the two months.

In January and February, country banks decreased their balances due from banks by $136 million more than the usual seasonal drop. They also allowed their excess reserves to decrease about $151 million in February, and they reduced their holdings of government securities by $462 million in January and February.

Thus the behavior of interbank balances in early 1951 contributed temporary but significant pressure upon the city banks as they were adjusting to their own increased requirements. Aside from very temporary heavy withdrawals, the movement of interbank balances took the form of a smaller increase than usual in January and a greater than usual drop in February. Country banks were able to shift part of the pressure upon their own reserve position to their city correspondents.

In 1953 and 1954 came reductions in reserve requirements in order to increase the availability of credit. In June, 1953, the Board of Governors announced a reduction of requirements by an estimated $1,156 million. This was to release reserves of $312 million at country banks on July 1 and then, on July 9, $499 million and $345 million at central reserve and reserve city banks respectively.[28] However, during the five weeks ending July 29, Treasury operations, together with other factors, tended to use up more than $600 million of member bank reserves [29] in spite of the supplying of reserves by Federal Reserve purchases on the open market and

[28] Board of Governors release, June 25, 1953: reprinted in "Decrease in Reserve Requirements," *Monthly Review* (Federal Reserve Bank of New York), July, 1953, p. 100.

[29] "Money Market in July," *Monthly Review* (Federal Reserve Bank of New York), August, 1953, p. 114.

expansion of discounts and advances. Thus only about $600 million of released funds were actually available for use by member banks, and a large part of these reserves was absorbed by the expansion of deposit liabilities and the resulting increase of required reserves. Deposits grew during July as member banks increased their loans and investments. The chief increase occurred in holdings of government obligations, which rose about $4.2 billion, with increases of $1,725 million by reserve city banks, $1,199 million by New York banks, $971 million by country banks, and $287 million by Chicago banks.

Country banks made only small and temporary additions to their correspondent balances as reserve requirements were reduced. Their average balances increased during July by $252 million, or by $78 million when allowance is made for the customary July upswing. In the following month, however, balances dropped, contrary to the usual seasonal movement, so that from June to August there was a slight drop of $33 million on an adjusted basis. At the same time country banks reduced their borrowing from Federal Reserve banks by $74 million during July while excess reserves increased $106 million; consequently, their free reserves (excess reserves minus borrowings at Federal Reserve banks) rose by $180 million.

Balances owned by reserve city banks showed little change during July and August. They declined $75 million, or $47 million adjusted, as a result of a smaller than usual increase during July and a larger decrease in August. Thus the reduction in requirements did not bring any accumulation of funds from reserve city banks to their correspondents. This reflects the tight reserve position of these banks as a group, for they were borrowing at Federal Reserve banks and their net borrowed reserves (borrowings at Federal Reserve banks minus excess reserves) were increasing.

Banks receiving interbank deposits gained only small amounts temporarily. The increase in balances on deposit with reserve city banks averaged $20 million in July on an adjusted basis ($233 million unadjusted), but August brought a decline of over $100 million. In Chicago, interbank deposits increased $20 million (adjusted) during July while little change occurred at New York banks.

The release of reserve funds in 1953 led to almost no sustained movement of interbank balances. Country banks did allow their balances (adjusted) to rise by about $78 million during July, but this was a temporary increase wiped out in August. Corresponding to the July increase in balances, slight gains in interbank deposits occurred at reserve city and Chicago banks. However, New York banks showed a smaller than usual flow of funds from correspondents. Thus in 1953 the existence of bankers' balances had little apparent effect upon the consequences of reductions in reserve requirements.

On June 21, 1954, came the announcement of another reduction in legal requirements, effective in steps from June 16 (retroactively) to August 1. Since the consequent freeing of $1,555 million of reserves would have brought a temporary overabundance of reserves, it was understood by the Board of Governors that the Federal Reserve System would absorb some of the released funds through the sale and redemption of Treasury obligations,[30] and, in July and August, Federal Reserve bank holdings of government securities were re-

[30] Board of Governors of the Federal Reserve System, *Annual Report,* 1954, pp. 88–89.

duced by $1,014 million. Largely as a result of these operations, total reserves of member banks in August averaged $1,055 million less than in May, and consequently the released reserves actually available during this period amounted to approximately $500 million, considerably less than $1,555 million. Of freed reserves, approximately $400 million was absorbed by the expansion of deposits from May to August, resulting from the rise of member bank investments, chiefly in government obligations.

Relatively small changes in interbank balances occurred during these months. Country banks increased their balances since they were slower than other banks in investing funds released by the reduction of requirements. Furthermore, their reserve position was easier to begin with and continued easier since Treasury redemptions shifted funds to country banks and Federal Reserve open market operations tended to place initial pressure upon central reserve city banks, especially those in New York, during these months.[31] Country bank balances due from banks, seasonally adjusted, averaged $168 million higher in August than in May and at the same time free reserves rose $215 million. Reserve city banks also added $34 million to their balances with other banks (adjusted), and their free reserves averaged $16 million more in August than in May. It was chiefly the reserve city banks which gained funds through movements of balances for their due to banks (adjusted) rose $188 million while those at Chicago banks increased by $67 million and New York banks suffered a loss of an estimated $32 million.

Thus the effects of the reduction of reserve require-

[31] "Money Market in August," *Monthly Review* (Federal Reserve Bank of New York), September, 1954, pp. 117–18.

ments in 1954 were somewhat redistributed through the movement of interbank balances. Country banks and to a much smaller degree reserve city banks accumulated part of their released funds in balances due from city correspondents. Chief gainers of interbank balances were the reserve city and Chicago banks, and their reserve position was thereby slightly eased.

In summary, experience since 1936 shows that interbank deposits have been one important means by which member banks have adjusted to changes in reserve requirements. However, adjustments have also taken other forms, such as the reduction of investment in government securities in 1951 or the increase in Treasury portfolios in 1954. In recent years Treasury obligations have been a more important means of adjustment and balances somewhat less important than in the 1930's, since correspondent balances have fallen to a kind of minimum needed for day to day transactions. Excess reserves have also absorbed part of the impact of changes in requirements, and lately the generally tight reserve position of many banks of each class has meant that borrowings rather than interbank deposits have been affected.

The use of bankers' balances has been a rather temporary method of responding to changes in reserve requirements, as in 1948, when funds returned to city correspondents shortly after withdrawals had been made. Even though brief, the resulting pressure has been severe because it has come at the very time when the required reserves of city banks have been increased. In recent years withdrawals have been made chiefly by country banks and much of the effect has therefore fallen upon reserve city banks. New York banks have been affected, too, because reserve city banks in turn have drawn down their own balances due from banks.

The predictability of the impact of reserve requirement changes is lessened by the existence of interbank deposits since the distribution of reserves among individual banks and classes of banks can be quickly altered through movements of interbank balances. The exercise of monetary control is thereby made more difficult.

4. Significance of Correspondent Banking

Having examined the size, distribution, and movements of interbank deposits, let us consider their significance. The result of our unit banking system, they have helped meet the needs of this system. Furthermore, correspondent relations are essential so long as membership in the Federal Reserve System is optional for state banks. Services provided by correspondents do duplicate those of the Federal Reserve banks in considerable part. On the whole this has not been inefficient or undesirable, and city correspondents render additional services that are not considered appropriate for Federal Reserve banks to perform. Interbank deposits have constituted a perplexing problem in connection with reserve requirements. The existing geographical basis for reserve classification is hard to justify and might well be abolished. However, there is some justification for separate reserve requirements against interbank deposits.

CONTRIBUTION TO THE SYSTEM OF INDEPENDENT UNIT BANKS

Multiplicity of independent banks is a striking feature of our banking system, in contrast to the extensive branch banking existing in such countries as Canada and the United Kingdom. In the United States neither branch banking nor group banking (achieved through holding companies or other devices) has developed a system of nationwide banks.

In recent years the number of branch offices has grown rapidly, but they are limited in geographical extent. At the end of 1955, there were 6,710 branches or other offices, which were maintained by 1,659 of the 13,716 commercial banks, but most of these branches were located near the head office.[1] State legislation and Federal regulation (which follows state restrictions) have limited the establishment of branch offices almost exclusively to the state of the parent bank[2] and frequently to the immediate vicinity of the head office. A few states prohibit branches. Therefore, in spite of the increasingly close interconnections of the sections of this country and the development of business firms operating on a nationwide scale, no widespread network of branch banking has developed, and unit banks have continued to be characteristic.

Correspondent banking fulfills many of the functions performed by branch banking in other countries, although it does so in a different way and in varying degree. Correspondent relations increase the mobility of funds. A temporary surplus in a country bank flows easily into the balance on deposit with its city correspondent, which may then utilize the funds. Local tightness of money because of heavy seasonal demands upon the country bank and the credit needs of large local borrowers may be met through the city bank's participation in loans. In addition, the correspondent relationship helps in the maintenance of liquidity since

---

1 *Federal Reserve Bulletin*, April, 1956, pp. 398–99.

2 At the end of 1955 all but six branches were within the state of the parent bank. *Ibid.*

the interbank deposit may be drawn down when the cash outflow from the country bank is heavy, or funds may be obtained from the city bank through borrowing, the purchase of Federal funds, or the sale of securities. Investment advice by those in close touch with the securities and money markets also increases the mobility of funds and contributes to the maintenance of liquidity. Assistance in meeting problems of bank operations is also offered by the city correspondent. Thus many of the advantages of branch banking are met, or partially met, by the correspondent system.

The real banking services offered by correspondents are not always fully utilized, and not all aspects of correspondent activities are of general economic benefit. Procurement of baseball tickets for bank officers, which was the only service reported by a city bank for one correspondent, is perhaps of doubtful general economic benefit. Correspondent relations may restrict competition for bank business. City banks may not give careful attention to the small bank's problems. Nevertheless, the correspondent system has contributed to the functioning of unit banking. Should our traditional policy of limitation of branch banking be changed, the correspondent network would largely lose its reason for being. Further extension of intrastate branches will lessen the need for correspondent banks and reduce their contribution to the functioning of the commercial banking system.

AN INTEGRAL PART OF OUR DUAL BANKING SYSTEM

So long as dual banking with optional membership in the Federal Reserve System is maintained, bank correspondents are needed. For many years state and Federal governments have each chartered and supervised commercial banks. This duality of authority is blurred by the existence of the Federal Reserve, since those state chartered banks that choose to become members of the System are subject to both Federal and state regulation. Furthermore, Federal deposit insurance includes most state banks. Nevertheless, if state banks wish to do so, they may remain subject to the exclusive supervision of the state, and national banks operate under Federal regulation only; thus the dual nature of banking is continued.

State banks which do not join the Federal Reserve System must rely upon correspondents for certain essential functions. Most nonmember banks hold part of their legally required reserves in the form of interbank deposits. It is through their correspondents that they clear out-of-town checks,[3] transfer funds, and obtain coin and paper currency. Correspondent banks thereby provide a connecting link between nonmember banks and between nonmembers and members, and they provide a channel to the source of supply of currency.

In their service to nonmembers, correspondent banks undertake certain of the functions of a central bank: the holding of legal reserves and the provision of circulating currency. In addition they are a source of credit to the nonmember bank. Yet these functions are not really analogous to those of a central bank in that the correspondent does not hold the ultimate reserves nor is it a bank of issue. The city bank relies (perhaps indirectly through a correspondent) upon Federal Reserve banks to supply its needed vault cash.

The correspondent system provides a link between the nonmember bank and the Federal Reserve System.

---

[3] However, nonmember banks are permitted to make clearing arrangements with Federal Reserve banks.

Through their correspondents, nonmember banks often benefit indirectly from Federal Reserve activities, such as check clearing, issuance of currency, and transfer of funds. However, nonmember banks do not ordinarily have access to borrowing at Federal Reserve banks, nor are they subject to the general monetary and credit controls of the Federal Reserve. Only indirectly through their correspondents and the money markets, do nonmember banks feel the impact of Reserve policies.

CORRESPONDENT SERVICES TO MEMBER BANKS

Certain activities of city correspondents duplicate those of the Federal Reserve banks, but such duplication of service is not necessarily undesirable. Both correspondents and the Federal Reserve provide facilities for clearing and collecting checks, a service in which speed and efficiency are of great importance not only to the banks themselves but also to the general business community. A joint comittee to study the check collection system was appointed in 1952 by the American Bankers Association, the Association of Reserve City Bankers, and the Federal Reserve System. After an extensive survey, the committee made recommendations looking toward the minimizing of the number of handlings of items and the improvement of the routing of checks for collection. While retaining both correspondent and Federal Reserve clearing as complementary systems, the recommended changes were designed to eliminate certain duplications which reduced the efficiency of check collection.

Other correspondent services likewise overlap those rendered by Federal Reserve banks, such as custody of securities, collection of noncash items, and wire transfer of funds, all of which are available to the smaller member bank. The Federal Reserve Bank of New York has for several years provided assistance to member banks on operational problems, as have correspondents. Nevertheless, both Federal Reserve banks and the large city correspondents can render these services well, and the existence of alternatives does not appear undesirable.

Member banks must rely upon correspondents for certain important activities which are not undertaken by Federal Reserve banks and are not considered appropriate to Federal Reserve functions. Member banks must use correspondents to provide foreign drafts and to make foreign collections. Investment advice is available through the correspondent. Credit information may be provided by the Reserve banks, but it is limited in extent and member banks themselves are the chief source of such information. Mobility of funds is provided by participation in loans, sometimes through excess loans originating with the local correspondent and sometimes through loans by the city correspondent in which the interior bank is invited to participate. Correspondents assist in the development of new business. These services which the correspondent performs are of great importance to the local bank and they are services which the Federal Reserve banks would not appropriately render.

INTERBANK DEPOSITS AND RESERVE REQUIREMENTS OF THE FEDERAL RESERVE SYSTEM

Correspondent banking and interbank balances are closely connected with the present structure of reserve requirements for members of the Federal Reserve System and with various proposals concerning a new basis for requirements. The existing structure, based upon location, reflects the historical development of correspondent banking in connection with bank note redemption and other functions. This was recognized in the national banking system by establishing higher reserve ratios for banks located in centers where other banks customarily maintained deposit accounts and by allowing banks outside the centers to count interbank balances as part of their legal reserves. The ultimate reserves then consisted of vault cash, and only this could be counted as reserve by banks in central reserve cities. However, at reserve city banks, part of the reserves could consist of balances due from banks, and at other ("country") banks a larger proportion might take the form of interbank balances. Although based upon location rather than directly upon the nature of the individual bank's business, this structure of reserve requirements approximated heavier requirements against interbank deposits.

The provision of bank liquidity was considered the primary function of the reserve requirements. Banks in the centers, which had traditionally been called upon to redeem circulating bank notes or to effect the transfer of funds for their out-of-town correspondents, were required to maintain higher reserves and/or higher percentages of reserve in the form of vault cash. The liquidity concept of reserves was carried over into the Federal Reserve System, which retained the classification of banks by location.

Over the years this geographical classification has been attacked and proposals to abolish it have been made repeatedly. Chairman Martin of the Federal Reserve Board of Governors has testified to the inequities and difficulties in the existing system of required reserves.[4] Location either inside or outside reserve or central reserve cities no longer indicates the nature of a bank's business, since banks in reserve cities may receive few interbank deposits while many "country" banks carry on an extensive correspondent bank business.[5]

A proposal by the Economic Policy Commission of the American Bankers Association made public early in 1957 (and after this study was completed but not yet published) would abolish geographical differences in member bank requirements and establish a uniform requirement against all demand deposits, whether interbank or other.[6] Other proposals have suggested the elimination of the geographical basis and substitution of differential requirements to be established according to the nature of the deposits at the individual bank. As early as 1919 the Federal Advisory Council recommended that classification be based upon the character of the bank's business.[7] In 1948 there was widespread discussion of proposals for geographically uni-

---

4 Congress of the United States, Joint Committee on the Economic Report, 82d Cong., 2d Sess., *Monetary Policy and the Management of the Public Debt: Replies to Questions,* Part 1 (1952), pp. 474–76.

5 Economic Policy Commission, American Bankers Association, *Member Bank Reserve Requirements* (New York: American Bankers Association, 1957), pp. 87–90.

6 Economic Policy Commission, American Bankers Association, "A Plan for Member Bank Reserve Requirements" (New York: American Bankers Association, 1957).

7 Federal Reserve Board, *Annual Report,* 1919, pp. 528 and 530. The Council, however, did not believe 1919 was an opportune time for adoption of this change.

form requirements with differential treatment of interbank, other demand, and time deposits.[8] The Douglas report to Congress in 1950 favored geographical uniformity with possible variation according to type of deposit.[9] In 1952 Chairman Martin suggested modification by authorizing the Board "to permit any bank in a reserve city or central reserve city to carry lower reserves . . . . where the bank's business justifies it (such as a relatively insignificant volume of deposits due to banks)." [10] This would be in keeping with the original philosophy underlying the existing structure of reserve requirements but would eliminate inequities among individual banks.

Although no longer generally regarded as the major function of reserve requirements, the liquidity concept of reserves still has significance. For the individual bank, reserves constitute a highly liquid asset and they contribute to its fundamental solvency. Thus, bank officers queried in 1952 concerning the chief function of reserve requirements frequently emphasized this aspect. "Many bankers believed that the only valid function of bank reserve requirements was the protection of depositors and the provision of liquidity for individual banks." [11]

For the individual bank, then, the liquidity concept of reserves has not been replaced; nor has it been replaced in state legislation or in the views of state super-

[8] Congress of the United States, Joint Committee on the Economic Report, 80th Cong., 2d Sess., *Credit Policies* (Hearings, April 13, 16, May 12, 13, 27, 1948), pp. 138–52.

[9] Congress of the United States, Joint Committee on the Economic Report, 81st Cong., 2d Sess., *Monetary, Credit, and Fiscal Policies,* Sen. Doc. No. 129 (1950), pp. 32, 36–37.

[10] Congress of the United States, Joint Committee on the Economic Report, 82d Cong., 2d Sess., *Monetary Policy and the Management of the Public Debt: Replies to Questions,* Part 1 (1952), p. 477.

[11] *Ibid.,* Part 2, p. 1168.

visors of banks. Replies to the 1952 inquiry showed that the "majority of supervisors felt that the principal function of reserve requirements was to provide liquidity for individual banks." [12]

Related to the historical conception of the greater liquidity needs of reserve city or central reserve city banks has been the belief that the higher velocity of interbank deposits requires higher reserve ratios than those against other deposits. In 1931 and again in 1934, the Federal Reserve proposed that requirements vary with the average velocity of deposits and that the formula be uniformly applied geographically.[13] Although the velocity basis for reserve requirements as a whole is no longer advocated, the idea of velocity remains in the background of thinking in connection with interbank deposits and appropriate requirements against them.

Data concerning the velocity of interbank deposits have not been obtained regularly. However, velocity in 1936 was computed for reporting member banks in 101 cities. The annual rate of turnover of interbank deposits at New York banks was 31 in comparison with 26 for reserve city banks, including Chicago, and 29 for country banks in other centers. The rate of turnover varied considerably from city to city but even more widely from bank to bank; velocity at some country and reserve city banks exceeded the highest rate at any New York bank. When cities were divided into financial and nonfinancial centers, interbank deposits at the former tended to show the higher rate of turnover.[14]

---

[12] *Ibid.*, p. 978.

[13] Federal Reserve Board, *Annual Report*, 1932, pp. 205, 260–85; *Federal Reserve Bulletin*, April, 1934, pp. 205–7.

[14] Victor Longstreet and Robert Fenn, "Turnover of Interbank Deposits at Reporting Member Banks in 1936" (mimeographed memorandum, August 22, 1938, Div. of Research and Statistics, Board of Governors of the Federal Reserve System), pp. 5, 9, 10.

Interviews with bank officers confirm the high activity of interbank accounts but indicate that certain other types of deposits, such as large corporate accounts and those closely related to the financial markets, are as active as interbank accounts. At New York banks in 1936, demand deposits other than interbank and United States government turned over, on the average, as rapidly as interbank deposits.[15] Velocity alone, therefore, appears to be an insufficient reason for separate, higher reserve requirements against interbank deposits.

Although high activity increases the risk of loss of funds because amounts withdrawn may not come back, balances in accounts which turn over rapidly may show stability from day to day or over longer periods of time. Therefore, volatility, which indicates not simply activity but susceptibility to sudden, wide fluctuation of balance, needs to be considered. If interbank deposits are more volatile than other deposits, higher requirements against them may be justified.

Interbank deposits as a whole and at many individual banks show regular seasonal variation (see Chapter 3). Fluctuations within the week or month are, also, likely to follow a pattern, reflecting habits of the public in making payments within the month and use by banks of interbank balances to adjust reserve positions. Such fluctuations, however, are recurring and can be roughly predicted and allowed for in the carrying out of loan and investment policies.

Other fluctuations which are irregular indicate volatility of interbank balances. In an attempt to obtain some measure of volatility, the variability of seasonally

[15] *Ibid.*, p. 10, and Victor Longstreet and Robert Fenn, "Turnover of Demand Deposits at Reporting Member Banks in 1936" (mimeographed memorandum, July 25, 1938, Div. of Research and Statistics, Board of Governors of the Federal Reserve System), p. 7.

adjusted monthly averages of daily figures around annual averages has been calculated for New York central reserve city banks in the period 1947–54. The coefficient of variation (the standard deviation of monthly averages as a percentage of the yearly average) shows the percentage range of average balances that could be counted upon by New York banks during a given year.

TABLE 23. COEFFICIENT OF VARIATION OF MONTHLY AVERAGES OF DEMAND DEPOSITS DUE TO DOMESTIC BANKS AND GROSS DEMAND DEPOSITS OTHER THAN INTERBANK
New York City Central Reserve City Banks, 1947–54

Year	*Demand Deposits Due to Domestic Banks (per cent)*	*Gross Demand Deposits Other Than Interbank (per cent)*
1947	1.2	1.9
1948	2.2	2.3
1949	1.3	0.6
1950	1.5	1.8
1951	1.7	2.3
1952	0.8	2.0
1953	1.2	1.1
1954	1.2	1.8

Source: Computed from data in the *Federal Reserve Bulletin.* Estimates of the due to domestic banks were derived from total interbank deposits by using weekly reporting bank data of deposits due to foreign banks.

Interbank deposits were not more variable than other demand deposits during this period as a whole (Table 23). The coefficient of variation for other deposits exceeded that for interbank deposits in six of the eight years and was considerably higher in three. This coefficient, therefore, gives no evidence that interbank deposits were more volatile than other demand deposits in New York banks during the years 1947–54.

For other banks or in other periods, however, interbank deposits may prove more volatile than other deposits. The behavior of bankers' balances in 1937 suggests that this may be true, especially at a time when balances consist of essentially idle funds not required for the day to day operations of the depositing bank.

Although the liquidity of reserves provides the historical basis of our reserve requirements, in recent years liquidity of the individual bank has depended rather more fully upon holdings of short-term government securities and the possibility of borrowing from Federal Reserve banks. Deposits in turn are protected by the Federal Deposit Insurance Corporation. In so far as they must be maintained at a minimum requirement, these reserves are immobilized and unavailable for meeting withdrawals (except that temporary deficiencies may be permitted).

Current emphasis is placed upon reserves as a means of implementing monetary policy. Through reserves, influence may be exerted upon the level of bank loans and investments, the general availability of credit, and the creation of deposits. According to the Economic Policy Commission of the American Bankers Association, "member bank reserve requirements today have little significance from the standpoint of contributing to bank liquidity but they have enormous significance from the standpoint of monetary management." [16] Thus Chairman Martin of the Board of Governors has said that "the most important functions of reserves and reserve requirements are now recognized to lie in their influence on the volume of bank credit and money and their role in monetary stability." [17] Chairman Harl

---

16 Economic Policy Commission, American Bankers Association, "A Plan for Member Bank Reserve Requirements," p. 9.

17 Congress of the United States, Joint Committee on the Economic Report, 82d Cong., 2d Sess., *Monetary Policy and the Management of the Public Debt: Replies to Questions,* Part 1 (1952), p. 464.

of the Federal Deposit Insurance Corporation, likewise, stated: "The function of bank reserve requirements is now, and for many years has been, control or at least strong influence upon the total volume of bank credit available for use as circulating medium." [18]

Reserve requirements do limit the expansion of bank credit and have served as a means by which monetary policy has been carried out for many years. The place of interbank deposits in reserve requirements must be considered, therefore, from the point of view of monetary control.

With the present structure of reserve requirements a shift of bankers' balances will likely affect the volume of required reserves for the banking system as a whole, and since total reserves are not changed by such a shift, the volume of excess reserves is altered. This follows from the differential reserve ratios between classes of banks and the provision that balances due from domestic banks may be deducted from demand deposits in the computation of required reserves.

The effects may be illustrated by considering the reduction of balances by country banks during the first half of 1937. If the entire reduction of $375 million had occurred at reserve city banks, required reserves would have fallen by about $22 million, and there would have been a corresponding release of reserves to the banking system as a whole. In so far as country banks withdrew from accounts at central reserve city banks, the release of reserves was larger, because of the greater differential in the requirements of country and central reserve city banks. The drawing down of balances owned by reserve city banks in New York or Chicago, likewise, reduced requirements and released reserves.

---

18 *Ibid.*, Part 2, p. 953.

The differential reserve requirements, therefore, make for a leakage in monetary policy. When the Federal Reserve Board raises reserve requirements, banks are likely to reduce their interbank balances and thereby release reserves, as was the case in 1937. Similarly, in response to Federal Reserve easing of credit, interbank balances may rise and bring about an increase of required reserves for banks as a whole. Consequently, movements of interbank funds may have effects directly contrary to those sought by the monetary authorities.

This leakage is not large, however. If we assume that, at the end of 1955, balances owned by country banks were all on deposit in reserve cities and those of reserve city banks were on deposit in central reserve cities, the complete withdrawal of these balances would have altered reserve requirements by merely $340 million.

The present arrangement, in effect, allows a credit against required reserves because of the due from banks. The size of the credit depends upon the reserve requirement of the owner of the balance; yet the amount of reserve held against the balance (held by the city correspondent) is determined by the ratio required of the city bank. The effect of movements of interbank balances upon the volume of required reserves could, therefore, be eliminated by allowing the depositing bank a reserve credit in amount equal to the reserves required of the city correspondent.[19] This change was included in Federal Reserve proposals in 1948.

In the carrying out of monetary policy, predictability of impact is lessened by the existence of interbank deposits. This applies especially to changes in

---

19 For illustration, see William R. Allen, "Interbank Deposits and Excess Reserves," *Journal of Finance*, XI (March, 1956), 70–72.

reserve requirements. In Chapter 3 it was made clear that considerable shifting in the location of reserves within the banking system occurs as a result of the movement of interbank deposits, and the impact of monetary policy actions upon banks may vary according to whether they are depositing or receiving banks. Thus, New York banks, or others carrying on a heavy correspondent business, may receive a double impact from Federal Reserve tightening or easing of credit conditions, once directly and then indirectly through the movement of their interbank deposit liabilities. This difficulty seems to be inherent in the correspondent system and not susceptible of correction through rearrangement of reserve requirements or otherwise so long as correspondent deposits continue as an integral part of commercial banking.

The separate classification of interbank deposits for reserve purposes may be desirable because of the attitude of the depositing bank toward its balances due from banks. Differentials between the several classes of banks are largely wiped out when total cash assets,[20] rather than legally required reserves, are considered. On June and December call dates from 1934 to 1954, country banks as a whole consistently maintained cash assets other than required reserves at a higher percentage of gross demand deposits than did reserve city banks as a group. In turn, reserve city banks maintained a higher percentage than did central reserve city banks, excepting only the Chicago banks in June, 1935. Thus the ratio of total cash assets to gross demand deposits does not show the same differential that is present in required reserves. Changes in the ratio were similar

20 Cash assets include reserves with Federal Reserve banks, cash in vaults, all balances with other banks, and cash items in the process of collection.

at all classes of banks, and after the war the ratios were rather uniformly maintained (Figure 11). From the standpoint of behavior, therefore, balances due from banks, together with vault cash or other cash assets, limit the expansion of deposits in much the same way as required reserves do.[21] This suggests, then, that there

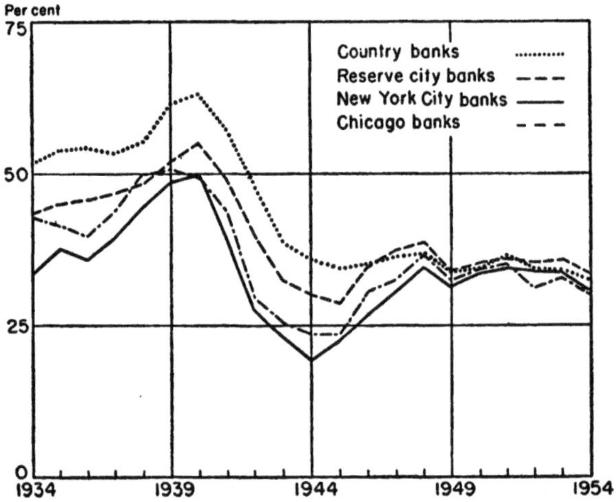

FIGURE 11. TOTAL CASH ASSETS AS PERCENTAGE OF GROSS DEMAND DEPOSITS
All Member Banks by Reserve Classification, 1934–54 at End of Year

Source: Board of Governors of the Federal Reserve System, *Banking and Monetary Statistics, Member Bank Call Reports,* and the *Federal Reserve Bulletin.* Beginning June 30, 1942, reciprocal balances are excluded.

is a close comparability between required reserves and other cash assets, such as interbank balances. If so, there may be reason to require larger reserves against these balances.

In conclusion, several elements appear to justify the

[21] A study of 201 country members showed that individual banks differed widely in their relative holdings of cash assets which are subject to control by banks; yet about one-half were consistent in their relative holdings, whether high or low. "Country Bank Management of Cash Reserves," *Monthly Review* (Federal Reserve Bank of Kansas City), August, 1956, pp. 5–6.

separate treatment of interbank deposits (or of banks receiving them) in establishing reserve requirements. First of all, interbank deposits constitute legal reserves of banks which are not members of the Federal Reserve System. This reduces the effectiveness of monetary controls since there can be multiple expansion of deposit liabilities of nonmember banks upon the basis of reserve deposits with member banks. The maximum bank credit possible upon a given reserve base varies with the size of bankers' balances owned by nonmember banks.

From the standpoint of monetary policy, therefore, it appears desirable that all commercial banks be subject to the same general requirements. In addition, the Federal Reserve Board has indicated that the differential in reserves required of member and nonmember banks has limited Board action in changing member bank requirements. This follows from the competitive disadvantages in which members would be placed by higher requirements and from the decreased attractiveness of membership in the Federal Reserve System. Extension of the same requirements to nonmember banks is not crucial, however, since their deposits are only about 15 per cent of the total for all commercial banks. Furthermore in a number of states, changes in requirements tend to follow those of the Federal Reserve System.[22] However, so long as the present dual structure continues, the holding of legal reserves in the form of balances with commercial banks would seem to justify special reserve requirements against these interbank deposits.

Second, interbank deposits are likely to be placed in

22 Congress of the United States, Joint Committee on the Economic Report, 82d Cong., 2d Sess., *Monetary Policy and the Management of the Public Debt: Replies to Questions,* Part 1 (1952), pp. 472–74.

larger banks in the centers of finance and trade. These banks are more sensitive to changes in credit policy than other banks and are likely to feel the impact of monetary policy more strongly. They are better able to respond quickly to changes in credit conditions and are more capable of full utilization of funds available to them. Thus higher reserve ratios may be justified upon the basis of the reduced expansiveness or contraction which this would involve.

In addition, there is some evidence that interbank deposits are more volatile than other demand deposits, as indicated by the heavy withdrawals in early 1937. Such volatility would warrant the maintenance of high liquidity on the part of recipients of bankers' balances. High reserve requirements against interbank deposits would lessen the need for highly liquid earning assets.

Two other points of rather different sort may further justify higher requirements against interbank deposits. One relates to the force of custom and existing practices. The saying that "an old tax is a good tax" points to the fact that the effects of an old tax (whether or not it is really a good tax) have been discounted and people have accommodated themselves to its impact. Our present reserve classification has long been in effect and, on the whole, the banking system has accommodated itself to such a structure. Thus there is merit in a reserve structure which does not depart too markedly from what has been able to function in the past. This point the Federal Reserve has made in terms of the practical problems of the dislocation in the banking system in shifting from one set of requirements to another.

Finally, in the view of the individual bank, balances due from other banks do have special significance from the standpoint of liquidity. They are part of primary reserves, along with deposits at the Federal Reserve bank, and they constitute a limiting factor in the expansion of deposits. Thus, special reserve ratios against interbank balances are warranted.

PROPOSED LEGISLATION

Legislation proposed by the Federal Reserve Board in the Spring of 1958 (S. 3603 and H.R. 11871) would make two changes of interest in this study: one would affect the reserve classification of certain member banks, the other would alter the differential requirements. Both appear desirable.

The proposal would broaden the Board's authority to exempt individual member banks from the higher reserve requirements applying in central reserve and reserve cities. At present a member may be permitted to carry lower reserves only if it is located in an outlying district of the city. The current proposal would make it possible to classify as a "country" bank an institution located anywhere within a reserve city and as either a country or a reserve city bank any member located in a central reserve city. This change would improve the reserve structure by allowing the nature of the individual bank's business to be taken into account rather than permitting location to limit the reserve classification.

The second change would reduce the minimum and maximum reserve requirements applying in central reserve cities to the same range, 10 to 20 per cent, that applies in reserve cities. Designation as a reserve city is based upon the size and importance of interbank deposits. Since reserve city banks have become increasingly important as receivers of interbank deposits, the need for differential requirements between these two classes of banks has diminished. Therefore, this part of the proposal is also desirable.

Bibliography

OFFICIAL PUBLICATIONS

Congress of the United States. Joint Committee on the Economic Report, 80th Cong., 2d Sess. Credit Policies. Hearings, April 13, 16, May 12, 13, 27, 1948.

——— Joint Committee on the Economic Report, 81st Cong., 1st Sess. Monetary, Credit and Fiscal Policies. Hearings, September, November, and December, 1949.

——— Joint Committee on the Economic Report, 81st Cong., 2d Sess. A Collection of Statements Submitted to the Subcommittee on Monetary, Credit, and Fiscal Policies by Government Officials, Bankers, Economists, and Others. Sen. Doc. No. 132, 1950.

——— Joint Committee on the Economic Report, 81st Cong., 2d Sess. Monetary, Credit, and Fiscal Policies. Sen. Doc. No. 129, 1950.

——— Joint Committee on the Economic Report, 82d Cong., 2d Sess. Monetary Policy and the Management of the Public Debt: Replies to Questions. 1952.

——— House of Representatives, 63d Cong., 1st Sess. Changes in the Banking and Currency System of the United States. Report No. 69, 1913.

——— House of Representatives, Committee on Banking and Currency, 71st Cong., 2d Sess. Branch, Chain, and Group Banking. Hearings, June 3–11, 1930.

——— House of Representatives, Committee on Banking and Currency, 78th Cong., 2d Sess. Hearings on H.R. 3956, Absorption of Exchange Charges, December, 1943, and January and February, 1944.

——— Senate, Select Committee on Small Business, 82d Cong., 2d Sess. Committee Print No. 7, Concentration of Banking in the United States, Staff Report of the Board of Governors of the Federal Reserve System Submitted to the Subcommittee on Monopoly. 1952.

Federal Deposit Insurance Corporation. Annual Reports, 1934–54.

——— Report of Assets, Liabilities, and Capital Accounts; Commercial and Mutual Savings Banks, June 30 and December 31, 1934–54.

Federal Reserve System, Board of Governors. All Banks in the United States and Possessions—Principal Assets and Liabilities, December 31, 1954. Release No. E (4).

——— Annual Reports, 1919, 1932, 1934–54.

——— Banking and Monetary Statistics, 1943.

——— Federal Reserve Bulletin, 1934–56.

——— Member Bank Call Reports, 1934–54.

——— The History of Reserve Requirements for Banks in the United States. Reprinted from *Federal Reserve Bulletin,* November, 1938.

NONOFFICIAL PUBLICATIONS

Alhadeff, David A., "The Market Structure of Commercial Banking in the United States," *Quarterly Journal of Economics,* LXV (1951), 62–86.

Allen, William R., "Interbank Deposits and Excess Reserves," *Journal of Finance,* XI (1956), 68–73.

American Banker. Annual reviews of correspondent banking. (Usually published about the middle of December.)

American Bankers Association, Economic Policy Commission. How our Reserve Banking System Operates. Monetary Study No. 2, rev. ed. New York, 1954.

——— Member Bank Reserve Requirements. New York, 1957.

——— A Plan for Member Bank Reserve Requirements. New York, 1957.

"An Analysis of Correspondent Bank Relationships," *Mid-Continent Banker,* XXX (February, 1934), 4–6.

Association of Reserve City Bankers. Correspondent Banking. Chicago, 1945.

Beaty, John Y. Correspondent Banking Is Important to Everyone on the Bank Staff. Bank Employees Library, No. 5. Cambridge, Mass., Bankers Publishing Co., 1951.

Beckhart, B. H., Julia E. Schairer, and Gail E. Sharpe. Is New York Losing Its Relative Position in the Banking Structure of the Country. New York, Chase National Bank, 1942. (Mimeographed.)

Beckhart, Benjamin Haggott, and James G. Smith. Sources and Movements of Funds. Vol. II of *The New York Money Market,* Benjamin Haggott Beckhart, ed. New York, Columbia University Press, 1932.

Bell, Elliott V., "Eccles Opposed on Deposit Plan," New York *Times,* December 18, 1938.

Bolthouse, Charles J. The Development of the System for Clearing and Collection of Checks. New Brunswick, N. J., 1939. (Submitted in partial fulfillment of the requirements of the Graduate School of Banking of the American Institute of Banking.)

Bopp, Karl R., "Commercial Bank Reserves—A Reappraisal," *Commercial and Financial Chronicle,* Vol. 168, November 4, 1948, pp. 1872, 1878–79. (Address before the 47th Annual Conference of the National Association of Supervisors of State Banks, Louisville, Kentucky, September 22, 1948.)

Carr, Hobart C., "Federal Funds," in *Money Market Essays,* pp. 13–15. New York, Federal Reserve Bank, 1952.

Chapman, John M. Concentration of Banking. New York, Columbia University Press, 1934.

Chapman, John M., and Ray B. Westerfield. Branch Banking. New York, Harper and Bros., 1942.

"City Banks Report on Correspondent Banking," *Banking,* XLVI (November, 1953), 35–38, 94.

Clayton, Lawrence, "The Federal Reserve System and Dual Banking," *Commercial and Financial Chronicle,* Vol. 170, September 22, 1949, pp. 1144, 1160–61. (Address before the Ninth Virginia Bankers Conference, Charlottsville, Virginia, September 8, 1949.)

"Correspondent Balances Show Gain," *Finance,* XLVIII (January 25, 1945), 17, 52–54.

"Correspondent Bank Relationship Study Results," *Banking,* XXXVIII (November, 1945), 64.

"Correspondent Banking is Real Big Business," *Finance,* XLVI (February 25, 1944), 7–8, 30–31.

"Country Bank Management of Cash Reserves," *Monthly Review* (Federal Reserve Bank of Kansas City), August, 1956, pp. 3–9.

Currie, Lauchlin, "Member Bank Reserves and Bank Debits," *Quarterly Journal of Economics,* XLVII (1933), 349–56.

Federal Reserve Bank of New York. *Monthly Review.* (Monthly articles on the money market.)

Finance. Annual and semi-annual surveys of correspondent banking.

Friday, David, "Legal Reserve Requirements: Are They Obsolete?" *Bankers Monthly,* XLIX (January, 1932), 33–34, 46.

Garvy, George. The Development of Bank Debits and Clearings and Their Use in Economic Analysis. Washington, Board of Governors of the Federal Reserve System, 1952.

Goldschmidt, R. W. The Changing Structure of American Banking. London, George Routledge and Sons, 1933.

"Group Banking: Twin Cities Answer a Need," *Business Week,* May 22, 1954, pp. 114 ff.

Hedges, Joseph E. Commercial Banking and the Stock Market before 1863. Johns Hopkins University Studies in History and Political Science, Series LVI, No. 1. Baltimore, Johns Hopkins Press, 1938.

Hoover, Calvin B., and B. U. Ratchford. Economic Resources and Policies of the South. New York, Macmillan Co., 1951.

University of Illinois, College of Commerce and Business Administration, Bureau of Business Research. An Analysis of Bankers' Balances in Chicago. Bull. No. 21. Urbana, University of Illinois, 1928.

"The Impact of Easy Money on Tenth District Banking," *Monthly Review* (Federal Reserve Bank of Kansas City), October, 1954, pp. 9–12.

Joint Committee on Check Collection. Study of Check Collection System. Report to the American Bankers Association, Association of Reserve City Bankers, Conference of Presidents of the Federal Reserve Banks, 1954.

Jones, Thatcher C. Clearings and Collections; Foreign and Domestic. Columbia University Studies in History, Economics and Public Law, No. 347. New York, Columbia University Press, 1931.

Longstreet, Victor, and Robert Fenn. Turnover of Demand Deposits at Reporting Member Banks in 1936. Memorandum, Division of Research and Statistics, Board of Governors, Federal Reserve System, July 25, 1938. (Mimeographed.)

——— Turnover of Interbank Deposits at Reporting Member Banks in 1936. Memorandum, Division of Research and Statistics, Board of Governors, Federal Reserve System, August 22, 1938. (Mimeographed.)

McDonnell, W. A., "Correspondent Banking Plays Vital Role," *Bank News,* May 15, 1947, pp. 26–27, 70.

Miller, Melvin C. The Par Check Collection and Absorption of Exchange Controversies. Cambridge, Mass., Bankers Publishing Co., 1949.

Mooney, George A., "Accord Is Reached on Bank Services," New York *Times,* December 2, 1951.

——— "Banks Challenge Reserve Inroads," New York *Times,* November 19, 1950.

——— "New Phase Nears in Bank Squabble," New York *Times,* December 3, 1950.

Myers, Margaret G. Origins and Development. Vol. I of *The New York Money Market,* Benjamin Haggott Beckhart, ed. New York, Columbia University Press, 1931.

Palyi, Melchior. The Chicago Credit Market. University of Chicago Social Science Studies No. 33. Chicago, University of Chicago Press, 1937.

——— "Should Interbank Balances be Abolished?" *Journal of Political Economy,* XLVII (1939), 678–91.

Peters, J. H., "Our Correspondent Banks Help Us Get Out of a Groove," *Bankers Monthly,* LXII (November, 1945), 507.

Popple, Charles Sterling. Development of Two Bank Groups in the Central Northwest. Harvard Studies in Business History, No. 9. Cambridge, Mass., Harvard University Press, 1944.

"Profits on the Hoof for Biggest Stockyards Bank," *Business Week,* April 21, 1956, pp. 124 ff.

"Reserve Requirements of Commercial Banks," *Monthly Review* (Federal Reserve Bank of New York), XXX (July, 1948), 71–75.

Riggs, Lloyd C., "City and Country Banks Work Together," *Bank News,* May 15, 1947, pp. 32–33, 72–73.

Rodkey, Robert G. Legal Reserves in American Banking. Michigan Business Studies, Vol. VI, No. 5. Ann Arbor, University of Michigan, 1934.

——— Sound Policies for Bank Management. New York, Ronald Press Co., 1944.

Savidge, Edgar T., "Interbank Relations in Financing Agriculture," *Banking,* XLVII (July, 1954), 65–68, 112.

Sayers, R. S. American Banking System. London, Oxford University Press, 1948.

"Speaking Frankly on Correspondent Banking," *Banking,* XLVI (October, 1953), 34–41. See also pp. 3 and 5.

Survey of Banking Industry in the Northwest and Record of Northwest Bancorporation as a Bank Holding Company. Minneapolis, Northwest Bancorporation, 1938.

Tippetts, Charles S. State Banks and the Federal Reserve System. New York, D. Van Nostrand Co., 1929.

Tow, Clarence W. The Changing Volume and Regional Distribution of Bank Deposits. Kansas City, Federal Reserve Bank, 1946.

"United Bank Offers Its Correspondents Participation in Insurance Plan," *Mid-Continent Banker,* XLI (November, 1945), 24, 42.

"Variations in Interbank Balances," *Monthly Review* (Federal Reserve Bank of Kansas City), June, 1955, pp. 10–12.

Via, Murray G., "Helping Correspondent Banks to Meet Farm Credit Needs," *Burroughs Clearing House,* XXXVI (July, 1952), 26–27.

Warburton, Clark, "Has Bank Supervision Been in Conflict with Monetary Policy?" *Review of Economics and Statistics,* XXXIV (1952), 69–74.

Watkins, Leonard L. Bankers' Balances. Chicago, A. W. Shaw Co., 1929.

Wengert, James J., "What Country Bankers Think about Services of City Correspondents," *Mid-Continent Banker,* May, 1949, pp. 52–53.

Westerfield, Ray B. Money, Credit and Banking. New York, Ronald Press Co., 1938.

"What Country Bankers Think of Their City Correspondents," *Mid-Continent Banker,* May, 1945, pp. 30 ff.

Willis, Henry Parker. The Federal Reserve System. New York, Ronald Press Co., 1923.

——— The Theory and Practice of Central Banking. New York, Harper and Bros., 1936.

Woolfson, A. Philip, "The Inter-bank Deposit Problem," *Bankers Magazine,* CXXXVIII (June, 1939), 475–78; CXXXIX (July, 1939), 9–12.

Young, Allyn A. An Analysis of Bank Statistics for the United States. Cambridge, Harvard University Press, 1928.

Youngdahl, Richard, "The Structure of Interest Rates on Business Loans at Member Banks," *Federal Reserve Bulletin,* XXXIII (July, 1947), 803–19.

——— Various Methods of Fixing Reserve Requirements. Federal Reserve Bank of St. Louis Banking Seminar VI, February 17, 1950. (Mimeographed.)

Index

Bei Fragen zur Produktsicherheit wenden Sie sich bitte an:
If you have any questions regarding product safety,
please contact:

Walter de Gruyter GmbH
Genthiner Straße 13
10785 Berlin
productsafety@degruyterbrill.com